*When Russia Came to Stay* invites readers into the heart of an American woman's private struggles as she learns to navigate the emotional undercurrents swirling up in the midst of the perfect storm of a new marriage, motherhood and live-in Russian in-laws all at once. It is the story of "how love came to stay" — as nourishing and vivid as a hearty Russian meal with garlic and fish, leeks and goat cheese, swilled down with strong spirits and the even stronger bonds of family and tradition. With unflinching honesty and a gift for anchoring her perceptions with sensory detail, Povozhaev chronicles her discovery of an anchor in the face of in-law, outlaw tensions seeming at times to overwhelm and sweep her personal freedom aside without a thought. It is a hopeful, joyful faith, a love willing to "endure all things;" one that grows and reveals itself, not by going it alone in a faraway cave, but by finding in the rhythms and relationships of daily life as an Orthodox Christian, a home in Christ, the source of a hospitality of such proportions that there can no longer be strangers.

         Stephen Muse
         Author of *When Hearts Become*
         *Flame* and *Raising Lazarus*

In this memoir, Lea Povozhaev addresses the subject of intercultural marriage with candor, realism, and hope. As her husband promised, Orthodoxy finally did "connect the dots" for them, but only after years of patient struggle. A must-read for anyone involved in or contemplating marriage to someone with roots in another culture.

         Katherine Bolger Hyde
         Editor and author

A heartfelt account of a young woman's spiritual and cultural journey. Lea Povozhaev has written a moving narrative of her discovery of Orthodox spirituality and the struggle to reconcile her Protestant

American upbringing and the Russian family she joins by marriage. It is a story of joy and sorrow, misunderstanding and reconciliation — illumined throughout by the author's increasing awareness of the mystical nature of the Church and the power of the Holy Spirit to unite us in love.

> Peter & Sharon Georges
> Founders and Directors, St. Nicholas
> Uganda Children's Fund

*When Russia Came to Stay*

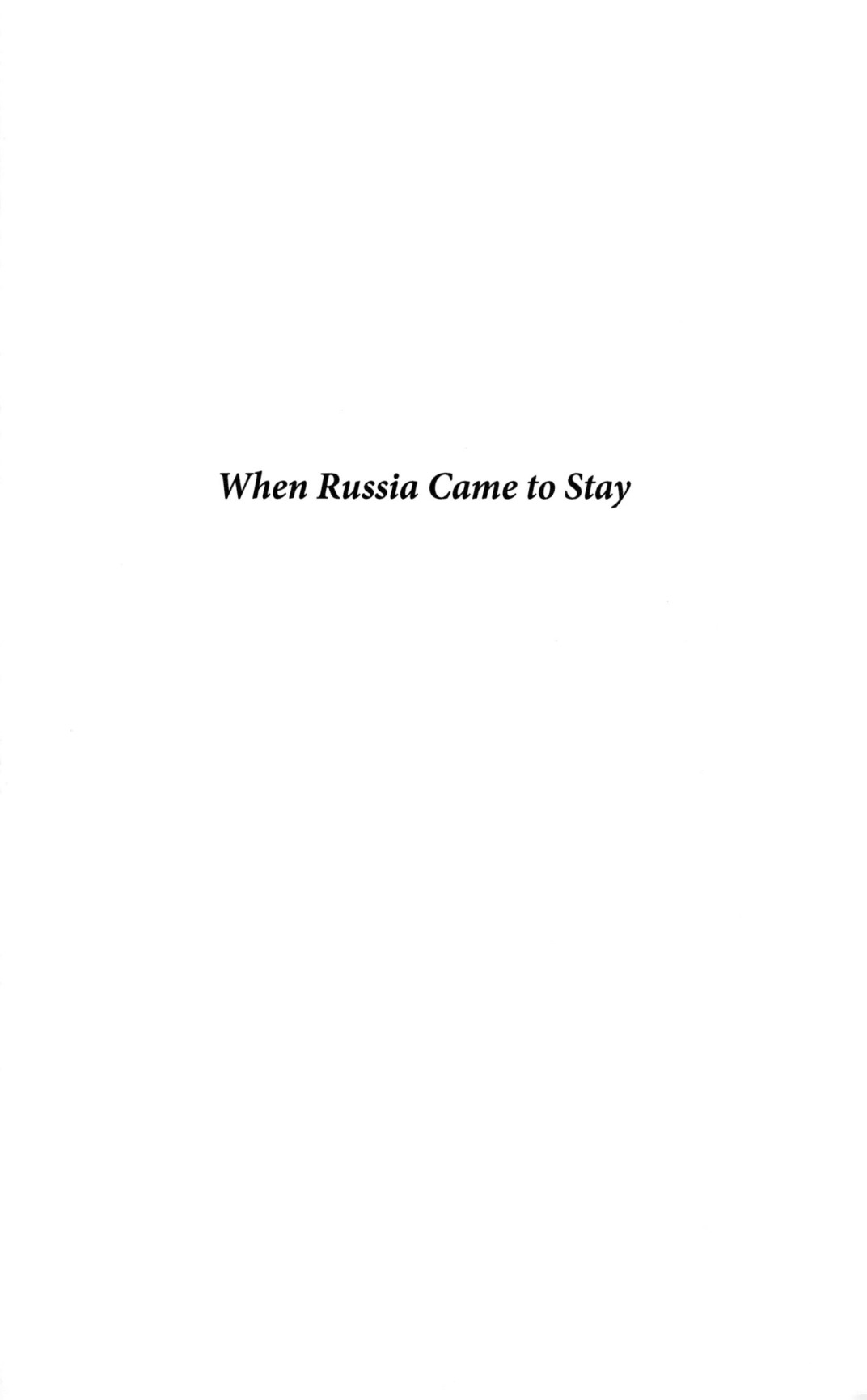

**Other books published by the Orthodox Research Institute include:**

Charles B. Ashanin. *Essays on Orthodox Christianity and Church History*

Rev. Dr. Steven Bigham. *Early Christian Attitudes toward Images*

David G. Bissias. *The Mystery of Healing: Oil, Anointing, and the Unity of the Local Church*

V. Rev. Fr. Sebastian Dabovich. *The Holy Orthodox Church: The Ritual, Services and Sacraments of the Orthodox Church*

V. Rev. Fr. Sebastian Dabovich. *The Lives of Saints: With Several Lectures and Sermons*

V. Rev. Fr. Sebastian Dabovich. *Preaching in the Orthodox Church: Lectures and Sermons by a Priest of the Holy Orthodox Church*

Margaret G. Dampier. *The Orthodox Church in Austria-Hungary: The Metropolitanate of Hermannstadt*

Protopresbyter George Dion. Dragas. *Ecclesiasticus I: Introducing Eastern Orthodoxy*

Protopresbyter George Dion. Dragas. *The Lord's Prayer according to Saint Makarios of Corinth*

Protopresbyter George Dion. Dragas. *St. Cyril of Alexandria's Teaching on the Priesthood*

Daniel Fanous. *Taught by God: Making Sense of the Difficult Sayings of Jesus*

Alphonse and Rachel Goettmann. *The Spiritual Wisdom and Practices of Early Christianity*

Fr. Stephen C. Headley. *Christ after Communism: Spiritual Authority and Its Transmission in Moscow Today*

Archimandrite Kyprian Kern. *Orthodox Pastoral Service*. Edited by Fr. William C. Mills

Matthew the Poor. *The Titles of Christ*

# *When Russia Came to Stay*

LEA POVOZHAEV

ORTHODOX
RESEARCH
INSTITUTE

*Rollinsford, New Hampshire*

Published by Orthodox Research Institute
20 Silver Lane
Rollinsford, NH 03869
www.orthodoxresearchinstitute.org

© 2012 Lea Povozhaev

All rights reserved. No part of this publication may be reproduced or transmitted in any form or by any means, electronic or mechanical, including photocopying, recording, or any information storage and retrieval system, without permission in writing from the author or publisher.

ISBN 978-1-933275-64-2

*Dedicated to Dima*

"The wind blows wherever it pleases. You hear its sound, but you cannot tell where it comes from or where it is going. So it is with everyone born of the Spirit." (John 3:8)

# Table of Contents

Introduction ................................................................. iii

PART I: FAMILY ........................................................ 1

    Chapter One
    *Dima's Past* ............................................................. 3

    Chapter Two
    *American Greetings* .............................................. 7

    Chapter Three
    *My Early Faith and Family* ................................. 11

PART II: FALLING IN LOVE ................................. 17

    Chapter Four
    *Meeting Dima* ...................................................... 19

    Chapter Five
    *Spreading Out* ..................................................... 27

    Chapter Six
    *Going into Russia* ............................................... 35

    Chapter Seven
    *Walking Deeper* .................................................. 49

    Chapter Eight
    *Unorthodox Worship* ......................................... 55

    Chapter Nine
    *Meeting the Parents* ............................................ 61

PHOTOGRAPHS ..............................................................................73

**Chapter Ten**
*Marriage* ................................................................................ 83

**Chapter Eleven**
*Changing Perspective* ........................................................ 101

## PART III: CONVERSION ............................................................115

**Chapter Twelve**
*Parents' Summer Visit* ....................................................... 117

**Chapter Thirteen**
*Emptying Our Nest* ............................................................ 147

**Chapter Fourteen**
*Baptism* ................................................................................ 169

## PART IV: SETTLING INTO FAITH AND FAMILY ....................183

**Chapter Fifteen**
*Baby Blues* ........................................................................... 185

**Chapter Sixteen**
*Staying Together* ................................................................ 203

## PART V: ABSORBED BY LOVE ..................................................215

**Chapter Seventeen**
*Our Fifth Pascha: Passover from Death to Life* ........................ 217

**Chapter Eighteen**
*Soul Laughter: Joy in My Heart* ............................................... 223

# Acknowledgments

For Jesus Christ and His saving love, echoing through each life in unique and splendid ways. For the increase of faith that comes with one's small efforts to cooperate in Him.

The mother of God endured separation from her Son after His crucifixion, though she longed to be freely reunited with Him. While on earth, she wore earthy colors, and I imagine her face a perfect icon of joyful-sorrow: an easy smile and deep-set eyes expressing longing and love. Though she daily prayed to be reunited with Him, she remained on earth to counsel the Apostles and to be Love to those she knew. She was over seventy when she fell asleep in the Lord. Christ came and resurrected her, and she intercedes for each in the world at the side of her Son. It is said that she is adorned with radiant colors in the kingdom.

This story is for the Theotokos, for the love that is easy to have for you. Thank you for making your presence known. May your help and protection guard those who seek God with their hearts, minds, and souls. May mothers who read this work, and all mothers included here, be edified and hear the call to be like you, however tiny our efforts are in comparison to the only ever-sinless one.

Thank you, mother of God, for praying for all Christians — always and forever.

Mom and Dad, thank you for always loving me and each other, for showing me that it isn't about being perfect but accepting one another and continuing to try to come together, whether it's easy or hard. Thank you for taking care of our home-life so that stress was never overpowering and home was truly a refuge. My sister Melanie, you are yellow and sweet. Thank you for answering my calls and replenishing my heart with simple prayers, hearty laughs, and, when close, a killer walk under a full moon.

For Dima, all of this, all of me, for better and for worse: always. Thank you for recalling calm and seeing outside of yourself. That you can sit on a bench on Mackinac Island and really see the birds, the water, and, more than see, feel the goodness of God by the majesty of nature—thank you. You teach me to pause and, literally, smell the roses. Thank you for encouraging me to go forth in faith. Thank you for the sixteen years we have shared since we were seventeen and first met, and for the future I pray we have together. May we build eternal treasures, weaving our family together in love. May we listen to God.

Thank you, Tatyana and Viktor, for having Dima, letting him come to America, and for choosing to live around the corner from our home in Ohio. This is your story also, and my prayer is for communication to increase between us. We have shared struggles; and while many of mine are voiced here, I hope you see the process of learning to love as one that is reciprocal with your own. May we rejoice in making it through so much and staying together as family.

For the Holmeses, though a pseudonym, you know who you are. I love you. Thank you for inviting, embracing, and sustaining our family. For all the occasions enjoyed with you in beautiful places, deep gratitude. More than the places, the things, beyond the education and occupations you've provided, thank you for the opportunities I have had to grow by you: through the willingness you show to people around the world. Thank you for the space you've always allowed for me and your many kind provisions. For you, Susan.

For all of my family. For Viktor and Dominik, your innocent witness of God's love, truth, and mercy. May this story provide perspective that, in some way, helps you when you're grown. This story has been in process since you were born, Viktor, six years before. May this time of reflection have been for good. Lord, have mercy.

# Acknowledgments

For spiritual guides and those who have helped me in the writing process, especially for Mary Mansur, Stephen Muse, Katherine Hyde, and Elizabeth LeMaster. Your attention to this work has helped in ways my own narrow vision could only view through your response. For fathers and mothers with whom I've shared, in some crucial ways, the journey of faith that led me into the Orthodox Faith: the Vollmans, Aunt Vicki, Pastor Klein, Calista, Kristen, Shelly, Ludmila, Sunchu, Jim, Fr. Nicholas and Matushka Elizabeth, and especially for the Georgeses and Fr. Andrew and Debbie. I love each of you in Christ.

I am also grateful for those professors that took time to respond and encourage the writing of a religious memoir in secular institutions: those in the NEOMFA and creative writing students at Walsh University. For Sara; for hope.

Versions of essays from When Russia Came to Stay have been published in a number of literary and spiritual magazines including: *Ohio Teachers Write, Sightlines, Fringe Magazine, Akros Review, America, Spiritual Life*, and the anthology *Growing Up Transnational: Identity and Kinship in a Global Era*, 2011, eds. May Friedman and Silvia Schultermandl. Additional essays from the memoir have appeared in a column in Cleveland State's *Vindicator* (2007–2010). Thank you to each publisher who has allowed my work to be in print.

Lastly, it is with great appreciation for Daryle Lamoureux and the Orthodox Research Institute that I conclude my acknowledgements. Thank you for your faith in this work. May God grant you great success in your endeavors with ORI.

Lea Povozhaev
Stow, OH
August 15, 2011
Feast of the Dormition of Theotokos

# Introduction

I converted to Orthodoxy from Protestantism five years earlier. My husband's grandmother had begun urging us to baptize our first son in the Church. Her plea came from Russia with love. Confusion and piqued interest led to phone calls to a priest, visits to parishes, and lingering questions about the life of a Christian. How was a young woman who had been raised Protestant in a middle-class, average family to become a wife, daughter, and mother in this multicultural family? With faith increased by the need to see God in the midst of our family's coming together, there was intense joy and sorrow. What follows is a story of coming into the Orthodox Church and becoming a multicultural family. It is a reflection on the circumstances of life that led to conversion and a testimony of love and hope in Jesus Christ, despite trying life situations. Faith ebbs and flows, but with the choice to believe and the will to sustain that choice there is renewal. This is a story for those who are in the world trying to live in Christ and love family. Particularly, it is for those seeking to stay together in marriage, to beat the odds against divorce, and to find the reward of sustained love. Dima and I come from vastly different cultures, and it is shared faith, and love that follows, that keeps us together.

I grew up in Mentor, Ohio, a suburb of Cleveland. The gray of northeastern Ohio hardly figured into those early years with my mother, father, and sister. We often walked down the street to Lake Erie: for cookouts, workouts, and graduation parties at a pavilion overlooking the water. Though there wasn't money for private piano lessons, our YMCA membership allowed for gymnastics and summer camps. Nana and Pop-pop, my father's parents, were rich in my young eyes. It was with them in Russell Township that Christmases and Thanksgivings were lush: pine, perfume, fires, and champagne. They were educated, well spoken; they allowed me the new and nice that seemed both less important and unobtainable with my parents.

Material and spiritual had always entwined in my conscious; there was the feel of fabric and the feel of prayer, and even as a child I wondered what each meant and how it should matter in life. My father's heart was for God. His words were few but real to me. In later years, I could see that his faith came from need to seek what was beyond money, education, and the good life his parents had worked hard to earn from meager roots. My mother's family was large. They were raised on white bread and Miracle Whip sandwiches, until my grandmother became an Evangelical Christian in her later years and redirected the family to healthier ways. My mother was the youngest of five children, and her parents passed on in my early childhood.

Growing up was gymnastics in summer dusk before baths. It was: "Now I lay me down to sleep. I pray the Lord my soul to keep. If I should die before I wake, I pray the Lord my soul to take." It was church in clean white places, public education until Evangelical college. At seventeen, I was trusting, secure, and interested when I met Dima, a boy from Russia.

He came to America at thirteen to play hockey. His parents remained in Russia until we married and they first visited. He spent his adolescence with the Holmeses, a wealthy host family twenty minutes from my home. Dima attended private schools and played on hockey teams as the quiet, easygoing Russian goalie. We went to separate colleges, and one semester I studied in Russia, met his parents, and first experienced the Orthodox Church. At this time, Dima could not return home.

Challenges came incrementally as the honeymoon faded, and reality with multicultural family was anything but predictable. Willing to work together, in Christ, we complemented each other, but we often frustrated our unity in failing to see beyond our own place. Though for years calm and quiet, Dima's passion emerged as strong as my own, and the fire in our marriage threatened to burn our family.

Dima and I were baptized with our first son the Christmas Viktor Jr. turned one. Nearly three years and our second son later, his parents came to live in America. Sometimes we went to church together. Faith was a quieter thing, often silent, with his parents. Its expression came in doing for one another. We tried. We failed. But life in Christ, found most fully in the Church, became the path to which we returned.

How did such unlike families blend and become one? There was no fine point answer to this lifelong inquiry. There were times when it seemed we were loving well, when raspberry vodka and hotdogs, bonfires and summer afternoons thawed traces of ice that continued to separate Dima's parents' world from mine. There were lesser times as autumn busied, phones were silent, and I hoped all was well with a distant family. And then there were occasions when dinner was dead cold, tensions burning silent.

Rooted in my mother's love, I was nourished even in dry times. She and my sister reminded me to give as they never stopped offering their calls, hugs, laughs and tears. Sometimes, distracted by my own life, I hardly saw others, but it was in seeing past myself that joy was possible. When I looked into Dima's gray eyes, now thirty-one, I saw his mother, his father, and felt the need between us. Though at times arms crossed his chest and eyes burned against my gaze, there was always love between us. While the passion could be exhausting, complacency would have been the end. We were at times fighting from different perspectives, but a protected seed of love continued to save us.

Encouraging my decision to become Orthodox was the belief that life in Christ spanned from the East to the West and that culture blended in the greater context of becoming Christian. The world was vast and varied, but there was order and purpose, meaning and truth. Like candles on Pascha night, bright ultimately illumined dark in all places and at all times. The faith Dima and I shared kept us together in dark times. The struggles, in light of Christ's saving love, were endurable and even the means whereby we changed for the better. The light was always there, though we didn't always see, and the Faith was the glue that kept us together.

# I

# FAMILY

"[S]tories are not memoirs but are life itself; they are the living source that gives you the strength to believe and to renew your ability to live…"\*

---

\* *Father Arseny, 1893–1973: Priest, Prisoner, Spiritual Father*, Vera Bouteneff, tr. (Crestwood: St. Vladimir's Press, 2002), 205.

CHAPTER ONE

# Dima's Past

From stories later shared, I imagine the family's earlier life in Russia. On a gray afternoon in Leningrad in 1976, people gathered by the Izhora River for the city's outdoor dance. Seventeen-year-old Tatyana wore a red coat, a thick braid between her shoulder blades. At twenty-three, Viktor had just finished his time in the military. He pushed his shoulders back and ambled to the shapely girl across the dance square.

"Excuse me. My name is Viktor Povozhaev." He offered her his arm. "Would you kindly accept a dance?" Her dark eyes contrasted the hazy day. She offered a nod and carefully looped her arm through his as folk music filled the air.

Tatyana had hoped to become a chemist or biologist, but instead of continuing her education, she chose to marry Viktor at eighteen. They lived in a typical Soviet apartment, concrete and old but made cozy with rugs and lived-in furniture. Dima was born in July of 1978. The apartment had one bathroom where Tatyana hand-washed their clothes in a black ceramic tub. The only bedroom was Dima's. A cat curled behind his skating trophies on the top of a wardrobe and ribbons lined the wall. The tiny kitchen held the indelible aroma of bread and sausage. On holidays, his mother set a card table in the living room with mix-matched china and lace linens. The living room also served as Viktor's and Tatyana's bedroom. They slept on a foldout couch below a Persian rug with cranberry and ivory swirls. As a baby, Dima often stayed with Grandma as his mother worked at a factory in the city and Viktor drove a bus in Leningrad.[1]

In Soviet times, religion was against the law. Many people continued secretly worshipping, but faith was quieted for over seventy-two years (1919–1991). Dima always knew his parents and Grandma believed in God. Perhaps it was in their simple ways of loving each other, though religion and faith were not explicitly discussed.

Dima stretched into a boy with skinny legs, a ball of a belly, and full cheeks. His gray eyes expressed emotions he never spoke. He began figure skating at four in the Kolpino Stadium, a government sponsored sports club with an Olympic-sized pool, full basketball and tennis courts and gymnastics equipment. The city hosted annual sports competitions and the wooden bleachers filled with eager spectators. Sports were taken very seriously in the Soviet Union as an opportunity to honor the nation.

Dima won first place in the city's four-year-olds' figure skating competition. In the competition the following year, he carelessly threw a fourth-place ribbon into his tote bag. His mother was quiet on the metro ride home, staring straight ahead at her round face reflecting in the window.

"Dima, why didn't you win first place?" she asked. They walked to their apartment, passing a small grocery with trash scattering in the autumn breeze.

"I thought I'd let someone else have a turn," he said, staring down at his sports shoes. He didn't want to disappoint his mother and loved the ice but wanted to play hockey. After practice one day, children played tag on the ice. Dima shifted his weight and lunged for a girl who had tagged him but instead tripped over her skate, landing with his head to her heel. When she pushed off, her blade sliced just below his eye. His mother's face drained of color as the doctor explained

---
[1] St. Petersburg was founded in 1703 by the then tsar Peter the Great. In 1914, the city was renamed Petrograd. After the death of Vladimir Lenin, 1924, the Soviet Union renamed the city Leningrad. After the fall of the Soviet Union in 1991, the city was again named St. Petersburg.

that the blade had just barely missed the eye.

Dima was seven when Mikhail Gorbachev ushered in political openness (glasnost) and economic restructuring (perestroika). His parents had food stamps, but the markets were without food. Women stood hours with their children for green bananas and bread. People grabbed what they could find. Even though Dima's parents were aware of the danger, as young as seven he stayed alone in the apartment while his parents worked. His father's words frightened him. "Don't open the door to anybody. Keep the door locked at all times, and stay in this apartment. You are to trust nobody." Dima glanced around the living room, listened to the silence, and double checked the locks. Black and white cartoons kept his fears at bay. He hunched over a small tray of hot tea and buttered bread and cheese and prayed for cartoons. *Nu Pogodi*, an animated tale with a wolf chasing a rabbit, similar to *Tom and Jerry*, bounced across the screen.

His father was engaged with his hockey training. It was warm enough by April to run miles around the edge of the park just outside the apartment, and they did dry land exercises to prepare for hockey season. The government sponsored summer hockey camps in rural Russia for four weeks of training. Camp was two days by train from home and surrounded by deep forest. The coaches and boys became like family, including hockey-stick cracks across bare bottoms when discipline was warranted, as was sometimes necessary dealing with young boys.

After summer hockey camp, Dima fell ill. He was sure the open window on the bus ride home resulted in his spinal meningitis. He spent a month in the hospital. After months of waiting, gray fluid cleared from his spinal cord, and within a year he was back on the ice. At first, he was weak and lost the position as starting goalie, but, as he often told me, "I'm at the top of my game when the odds are against me. I love being the underdog when no one expects anything."

In 1990, Mentor's Youth Hockey Program invited Dima's Russian team to the States for an international tournament minutes from my home. He played well in the tournament, even though he was small and not yet thirteen, and was invited to return to the States. In 1991, the year President Boris Yeltsin officially dissolved communism, Dima came to live in America.

Before he left Russia, he held his mother's hand in silence as they filed off the train and walked to St. Isaac's Cathedral in the center of St. Petersburg. It was the largest church in the city and one of the biggest domed buildings in the world. He felt tiny and inched closer against his mother's wool jacket. Her face was statuesque as they entered the museum. Perhaps she hoped to impress upon him Russian culture and history, which had always stemmed from the peoples' unquenchable faith. His mother said the church took forty years to construct and was open from 1818 to 1858. She looked ahead to the elaborate icons at the front of the church. They stood before an icon of the mother of God and she prayed.

## CHAPTER TWO

# American Greetings

Dima and his parents slept at the airport the night before he left St. Petersburg, Russia for Cleveland, Ohio. After fourteen hours and a time zone eight hours behind his parents', he was called to customs in New York's JFK Airport. An officer rattled through English as Dima nodded, "uh-huh, uh-huh," clueless.

He shuffled through the terminal, duffle bag filled with all he owned: three pairs of socks, underwear, and T-shirts, one pair of jeans and sweatpants, hockey pads and a stick. Underwear was worn a couple days before it was changed, and socks could withstand nearly a week's use before his mother had to wash them. Though crusted in dried sweat from the practice the day before, he'd shake the socks limber and put them on.

He had five hours before the flight to Cleveland, but time had ceased to exist for him — he would be in America for a year. Just over five feet tall in warm-up pants and a Kolpino hockey T-shirt, he blended as a nondescript part of Cleveland's airport. He watched closely as a maze of burgers and french fries, soft cookies and pretzels revealed to him a delicious America.

"Jerry Holmes," said the man, wire rimmed glasses perched on a smooth face. He stood straight, back nearly arching back, and extended his hand. His words were blank sounds rushing past Dima's ears. He followed Jerry in silence to a blue Mercedes. He had never been in a new car and had only ridden in a car a few times back home, always in the backseat. Jerry motioned with a firm hand to sit up front.

After a quick half hour coasting through Cleveland and into suburban Willoughby Hills, the car climbed the steep drive and glided under a canopy of autumn leaves partially illumined by the small lights along the driveway. A stairwell led to ridged pillars guarding a carved white door. Jerry curled around an island of ivy, lily-of-the-valley, and ferns and into the garage underneath the castle. There was a basketball hoop just behind the house. Mr. Holmes backed the blue Mercedes next to his wife's maroon one. He and Dima walked into the house through the basement door and Dima thought they were remodeling. Starched cloths and various ceramics, ornaments, and glass figurines filled the basement. A middle-aged woman, gray braid over her shoulder, looked up from her novel with soft blue eyes.

Caroline was an artist at heart, always crafting things. She had an eye for beauty and could transform a broken ornament into a valuable antique. She lived in her parents' old bungalow but had long ago outgrown it with her many antiques. During the seasons when Jerry traveled the Far East entertained by his business partner and observing the progress of their electronics company in Hong Kong, Caroline stayed with Susan in his basement. Jerry and Susan both loved people and did much for them. Family and friends from around the world stayed at the Holmeses' from time to time. There was always an air of remarkable generosity there.

Caroline and Susan were lovers of many things. They fought for the weak, for the silent. They pleaded with a neighbor not to cut down pine trees dividing their properties. They petitioned to save the old neighborhood bridge, though the city tore it down. They salvaged stray cats, nursed crippled birds, sewed, pressed, and painted what my mother might have thrown in the trash.

When Dima and I began dating, my family was invited for holiday meals at the Holmeses'. On one occasion, Aunt Caroline asked my father, "What have geese ever done to anybody? They are kinder than human beings." Typically, my father honked his horn and cursed the beasts as they sauntered across the street. Dad smiled and nodded.

Dima followed Mr. Holmes upstairs for his first night there. Jerry gestured around the kitchen and spoke slowly, "Are you hungry?" Dima shook his head and they walked past a bathroom into the front vestibule. To the side was a grand piano with pictures of two boys just a few years younger than he was. They mounted steps to a hallway of bedrooms. Jerry's and Susan's were to the right, and Jason's, Jeremy's, and now Dima's were to the left of the stairwell. He hauled his bag over the wood floor and glided his palm over English books stacked on a dresser. He looked in empty drawers, breathed the woody scent of the empty closet, and eventually pulled back the covers, eager for morning.

The beginning of this new life in America was challenged by more than the language barrier. He soon learned American children had limitations and expectations that he hadn't experienced with his parents busied by work and in a culture where education often ended by eighth grade. He wasn't allowed to stay home alone through the night. Education was to be first priority, superseding hockey, which had seemed his lifeline since he was four years old. And there were myriad other differences in the ways parents and children related to one another. Russian parents expected silence and obedience, which could seem unreasonably strict. American parents often allowed children more voice, sometimes more presence in their lives, which could seem rude and disrespectful. Quiet was natural to Dima's introverted character, but silencing too many thoughts and feelings took its toll.

During hockey season, the team traveled every weekend for eight months, played two to three local games during the week, and practiced each morning before school. Dima's American peers seemed nice, even helpful. When he asked how to say "pass the pizza," someone would slowly pronounce inappropriate phrases, which he learned well and easily retained.

Before coming to the States, he had never been out to eat. In the beginning, it was awkward when the server approached. He got his burger and french fry order down, and, with little exception, this remained his selection. These foods were not unlike the fried potatoes his mother made at home or the *catletta*, beef patties, fried with butter and onions, that he had often eaten. The buns in the States, warm and chewy, were sweeter than the dark bread he was used to. McDonald's easily became his favorite restaurant for its best burgers and no servers.

The team and parents went out to eat what must have seemed constantly to a boy from a family that never had. On Fridays, thirty people would go to Lucio's for pizza and iceberg lettuce under a blanket of mozzarella. The Holmeses took the team to a Samurai restaurant where Asian chefs flipped shrimp in the air and caught them in a sizzling skillet — red peppers, scallops, and mushrooms hissing. Sodas came with little umbrellas and American and Canadian flags, which Dima collected for his new baseball cap.

The lifestyle the Holmeses provided for Dima was so exciting he hardly had time or attention for anything other than the sheer fun of it. His first year in the States, he grew nine inches and learned much English. Life seemed beyond description. He could eat anything he wanted and was even forced to eat broccoli, spinach, squash—there seemed a limitless source of food. He could play video games for hours. While things went from one ripe banana to the next (bananas were second only to burgers), there were times he was homesick. There was a new silence to get used to. Sometimes he wished to hear his father's encouragement. His father was aching to be with his son once again. He'd stop in Kolpino's Sports Complex, other fathers and sons engaged in drills, and blink away his tears.

## CHAPTER THREE

# My Early Faith and Family

A child's heart is open and willing for the love of God. In my late childhood, just before hormones complicated the obvious, the supernatural world was real. I sensed the world was deep and layered and flowed beyond. I looked through life for God. Though there were seasons that were more and less intense, it seemed there hadn't been a time outside of this perspective. Perhaps conscious faith began when I was three and my father prayed with me for Jesus to come into my heart. Growing up, my parents' simple way of life, daily engaged with nature and not cluttered by too many material things, revealed a base of faith to me. They clearly loved each other, God, and me, in good and bad times. There was a goodness and truth in my parents that nurtured me throughout the years, especially in unsettling times.

My mother was from a family of people who would have garage sales on summer afternoons as an excuse to visit with the neighbors. Some of Mom's family was involved with church, some with cards, but they all loved people in an open, easy way that didn't seem to come naturally for my father's side of the family. Growing up, family had been my mother's religion. She was the youngest of five children in an average 1950s household. Her mother worked in the home, sold Avon, and volunteered at the local Protestant church. Her father worked at Arthur Pontiac and gave my grandmother a generous allowance for groceries. She kept the change and sneaked the children tens, sometimes twenties.

My mother is one day older than my father. They were raised in Cleveland Heights, Ohio and attended the same grade school. "Don Patton" had become a household name at my mother's, the crush that lasted through the years, even though the sum of their dating had been a few weeks in eighth grade.

It was the seventies. My mother's blond hair parted down the middle, poker straight. Polyester bell-bottoms clung to her long bones, hugging a fresh rose tattoo on her hip. She smiled broad and easy. Diane Bishop, the nice girl in the back row of class. My father's draft card expired in 1973, the year my parents graduated high school. As Vietnam continued two more years, my parents found their way back together. It was after high school graduation when my father needed a date to a New Year's Eve party and thought to call my mother. I count this a miracle in itself. When my mother announced she would be going out with my father, "Don Patton's from a good family," was all that my grandfather said as he lowered his combover back to the newspaper.

My grandmother folded my mother against her polyester blouse, Pond's Cold Cream and Noxzema tempering my mother's dizzy excitement. "Oh, honey. I'm so happy he called. The Lord's timing, the good Lord's timing."

They married at twenty-one and lived in Boca Raton, Florida. My mother's cheekbones were high and pronounced, and a bright smile lit her face. My father's hair was dark then, like a helmet lining his tanned skin. He talked about newlywed days. "Listen, we'd take bike rides in the middle of the night when we lived in Florida, and it was gorgeous. But I had to bring your mother back to her family. I tell you, you marry the entire family. Mark my words."

My mother would add, "Donny, we didn't have a cent to our name. Don't you remember those night shifts at Moe's restaurant? It's easy to romanticize those earlier days—"

"It wasn't so bad, Diane. We were in Florida." He seemed to drift from Ohio winter with the memory of palm trees, beach, and ocean. The trace of a scowl returned. "Working in the shop back in Ohio was no picnic—ten hours on my feet, handling screaming metal, blaring heat." My father would often say that life had never been what he had expected, not at any time along the way. In later years, my father seemed less bothered by unexpected turns in life and more aware of the importance of relationships. Though people seemed to have often wanted relationship with my father, he began to reciprocate in later years. It was most apparent in the ways he appreciated family. My father's attitude changed. Instead of teasing the young engineers at work, he began talking with them, listening. My father's faith seemed to change his relationships with others.

For my father, art was a way to focus energy and make something concrete. Fish mounted his basement walls — Rainbow Trout, Smallmouth Bass, Perch. "It's my showroom," he'd say, pushing the old couch further from the wall to hang a speckled fish. He was up at five and could spend full days in his faded Lincoln Electric shop coat, reading glasses halfway down his long nose, bowed over a stained table. He'd have a cup of weak coffee beside old canisters of Metamucil and Folgers Coffee refilled with plaster and paint.

"Your mother doesn't understand. But you understand. It's something you just have to keep working on. You're driven like I am," he'd tell me. My father and I connected through art and faith, and in some moments my soul seemed peeled from his.

My grandmother was diagnosed with breast cancer in her mid sixties, a month before my birth. While the news was shocking, the family hoped she would beat the disease. She was healthy, strong. My mother had little time to mull over the tragedy in the beginning. Her water broke three months earlier than the doctors had expected. I was racing into the world, which would remain a mark of my character through the years. After the emergency cesarean, I was the size of a palm and weighed four pounds. The first week of my life was spent in the hospital. I was a fragile swaddle of pink in my mother's arms when my father drove us home in the old Nova.

At the first baby well check, the doctor carefully told my mother that I had a heart murmur. "It's likely she has a hole in her heart," the doctor said, probing my chest. "Often when the infant comes early like this, she hasn't had enough time to develop fully in the womb. She just needs some extra attention outside of it," he looked into my mother's crumpling face. They shuttled us over to Rainbow Babies and Children's Hospital in Cleveland. My mother leaned over my jaundice face, wiping her cheeks with the edge of a blankey swaddling me.

My grandmother didn't ask my mother to pray with her, but I believed she never stopped. She told my mother I was on a prayer chain at her church. Perhaps my grandmother was grateful but not surprised when my heart healed without surgery, but my parents needed a way to express the mystery. To my mother, my grandmother's faith had seemed another extension of her nature, akin to psychic readers from years earlier. Her belief had seemed zany, overboard, like healthified cookies and cod liver and orange juice. A spiritual health kick. There was something beyond this, though, and it was felt in my grandmother's love. When she was dying, she continued the same as she always had—asking the family how they were feeling, listening to the details of their lives, when she wasn't in debilitating pain and exhausted by the cancer treatments. She tended to the family's worries, repeating that she was fine, silently confident in the Lord's plan, even if it meant death. Yet, her voice must have been heavy as she pleaded with my grandfather.

"Leonard please, accept Jesus as your personal Savior." It was the first and last time in over forty years of marriage that she had pushed the issue of faith.

"Oh, Matty. I've always believed in God. Why —"

"I know, I know," the words rolled slowly. She was calm and believed the Lord would save her family. "Will you say a prayer with me?" My grandfather echoed her in the "Sinner's Prayer."

When my grandfather passed away ten years later, my mother clung to hope for his salvation on account of this prayer. She studied his drained face, a bleached shadow of her father. He stared ahead and drifted into death. My mother believed he saw something more than she and the family could.

The deaths of my maternal grandparents unhinged the togetherness of the family. As my mother's own young family grew, holidays and special occasions were spent with my father's family. My sister and I shopped with Nana in department stores that smelled sweet. Ladies with bright lips sprayed perfume on our wrists. We came home to model our Christmas dresses for Pop-pop who whistled as we twirled and laughed. We hurriedly changed into old jeans and headed outside to build a snowman with Pop-pop. Nana and Pop-pop watched a golf tournament on the television, and we ate peanuts and Pringles before dinner. After roast, mashed potatoes and gravy, buttery corn and warm applesauce, we'd cuddle on the red couch and watch a movie.

It was a silent understanding that politics and religion would be avoided at Nana's. My Aunt Lorri was beautiful with deep green eyes and an energy that swung up and down. She said what she thought and seemed confident and intelligent. She'd sneak us bananas and chocolate before dinner as we built block forts.

With my father's family was art lessons, singing, and education. Nana corrected me as I told stories of my friends and me, "My friends and I," she'd say. They listened with attention and interest to the details of my life. I loved sharing bath time with Nana in her pale green bathroom, sorting through her red lipsticks, watching her powder herself. She was a nurse, Pop-pop an engineer, and my aunt held a Ph.D. in Nutrition. Their interests and talents inspired my own. Though we didn't talk about God in the same outright manner, we shared love and closeness, and I was happy and assuming mutual faith when Dad suggested I say the prayer before Christmas dinner.

My parents continued a pattern of trying to settle in and ultimately leaving a variety of Protestant churches. We moved to a new neighborhood down the street from my parents' friends, Peter and Sharon Georges. They lived in a matching house—split level on a postage stamp lawn. The Georgeses had become Orthodox after leaving an Evangelical church my parents had also attended. Their conversion seemed bizarre and foreign to my parents. Peter and Sharon home schooled, played the piano, and seemed cultured in ways my family wasn't. Perhaps their new church was an extension of a classical way of life. I savored the starchy smell of their home, slick piano in the corner, and books lining their basement walls.

The Georgeses sat at our kitchen table. Dad said, "You guys really like the Orthodox Church?" Peter looked up from my mother's date bread and nodded.

"I'll tell you what, we made a list of churches to try. The Orthodox Church was one on the list. I was raised Greek Orthodox, so why not go back and just retest the waters — right? Growing up, the parish had seemed an ethnic community — you were Greek, so you were Orthodox. It hadn't seemed about faith to me. I'm sure there were many for whom it was about faith, but I hadn't sensed that at the time. But the Divine Liturgy was in English at St. Nicholas, and there was just something that felt real there."

Sharon's eyes glowed. "We knew we'd be back," she said.

"It's true. It was like a light went on. I knew the Orthodox Church would be a place to stay," Peter said.

Sharon smiled at my mother. "I felt the reverence that had been lacking at many churches. It felt more complete. Diane, you'd love it if you just gave it a chance." My mother pulled coffee mugs from the cupboard and poured boiling water over instant coffee. The Orthodox Church was for foreigners, she thought. Without my parents knowing it, the Georgeses prayed, continuing over twenty years, for our family to draw into the Church.

## II

## FALLING IN LOVE

Love is a patchwork of days.
Patterned and colored, mended and promised
with gentle hands of hope.
Love is unexpected —
turning corners, treading paths where lilies-of-the-valley
    breathe.
Love is acceptance and peace.
The soul becomes in her embrace.

CHAPTER FOUR

# Meeting Dima

A short time before Dima and I met, I stared out my bedroom window at the dulling oranges of sunset and whispered, "God, if you are here, if you are really part of my life, I need a sign." Nothing changed. I barely breathed. There were no mountains to move. Only postage stamp yards, empty sidewalks curling the cul-de-sac, and silent street lamps. Across the street was a long yellow light in the shape of a cross. Just a porch light. The dark of night blanketed the earthy smells of grass and dying heat. Just the end of a day. And yet hovering inexplicably near was the sense that in and through all of this was God. I drew my breath, still as the old tree across the street.

I met Dima at seventeen on a blind date arranged by my sister's high school sweetheart and later husband Joe. Dave Matthews pulsed through the minivan as Joe drove us to the Holmeses' along winding country roads.

My palms were moist as the minivan lumbered up the drive to the house on the hill. Ivy spilled over the earth and front stairwell. An American flag hung between white pillars. The doorbell chimed classical music. I waited with a tight stomach when the door opened to the smell of Chinese vegetables.

"Come on in. The boys are upstairs." Susan Holmes reminded me of Martha Stewart relaxed. Her face was kind but reserved. She wore little makeup and small wire rimmed eyeglasses. She wiped her hands on a wide apron and motioned us upstairs. An enormous chandelier hung from the ceiling. Pink and silver wallpaper flowered behind Oriental statues of birds, monkeys, and lions. Red ribbons and orange dragons were set on shelves and a basket of dark walking canes was under a bronze icon of Christ.

The scent of Dove soap hovered in the hall. Dima stood there, tall and thin, an untucked Grateful Dead teeshirt over khaki cutoffs frayed just above pale knees. His face was hidden in the shadow of a baseball cap. I felt his boyishness as we sat next to each other in the dark minivan. Joe drove to Bob Evans. We looked out the window, at the backs of Melanie's and Joe's heads, at our hands — anywhere but each other. Yet I sensed something still and steady about him, and ease slowly replaced nervousness. Joe and Dima talked about the Red Wings game, and I listened to an unfamiliar accent. His body seemed fluid, and he didn't fidget or waste any movement. He hunched over, resting elbows on long thighs, hands on knees. Joe open the side door and Dima's long body folded out. I bent from the van into the spring night, eyeing Dima's soccer shoes. The air was light and almost cool. I wiped clammy hands on my stonewashed jeans and pulled at the cropped top as we walked into Bob Evans.

Melanie and I giggled over pie while the boys chatted. Dima was shy, reserved. The top of his cap faced me as he leaned over to sip from a straw. His arms were white and slender but not skinny, hands neat and angular. His eyes were light. We returned to the van where Melanie and Joe held hands and spoke softly. Dima and I turned to each other, and he held steady and direct his attention, not in intimidation but rather gentle confidence. His face was nearly childlike. We spoke of high school and sports, my running, his hockey, but it wasn't what we said that mattered as much as how we responded to one another. It seemed there was no pressure to impress, no hurry, no expectations. It felt as though we were inside a common place. With a gentle smile, he seemed sincere and respectful.

With time, I liked Dima more and more — the way he laughed noiselessly with the bob of his shoulders, mouth open. I liked the way his thumbs slid into his pockets, hands relaxed on his thighs; the way he almost looked at me, reserving his full attention. I sensed a protected distance that made me want to draw nearer. He was the first person I'd known with quiet resolve. To my family, voicing our opinions and thoughts and arguing others' was easy, but so was saying I love you. Mutual understanding was expected and usually came easily. With Dima, our differences were obvious and yet seemed to draw us together.

A relationship with Dima swept me into the Holmeses' household, and they began to introduce me to life beyond Ohio and America. The Holmeses' parties were many, and they weren't catered by potluck. There were dinners on china with Jerry's business partner from Hong Kong; Chinese New Year parties where guests cooked duck, sesame, and ginger stir fries in woks. They had gift-giving extravaganzas over Chinese takeout after Jerry's trips to the Far East, passing out gadgets like digital cameras or colored massage beads. We celebrated Christmas the entire day, gifts opened into the evening, Jeremy and Jason still in their pajamas (Dima changed for my benefit). There was an Easter egg hunt. Dollars and silver were stashed in plastic eggs tucked behind flower pots, in bird's nests, and lining fence ledges along the Holmeses' expansive backyard.

I was welcomed and felt Jerry and Susan trusted me from the beginning. Susan and I went together to her Lutheran church, to a teacher convention, to a Russian tea house. She drove through Amish Country where we stopped at shops in barns. The Holmeses' lifestyle was adventurous and added intrigue and opportunity to Dima's and my relationship. As we fell in love, his being Russian hardly figured in.

Dima learned what a close-knit, middle-class American family was like as he entered mine. Every time he ate over, my mother happened to be warming leftover casseroles. She worried, asked him if he thought dinner was awful, vowed to cook his favorite meal, but he quietly said dinner was good, he liked to eat anything, and slipped from the center of attention as easily as he had entered into it.

After leftover chicken tetrazzini, the noodles baked crunchy at the ends, we left my mother's embarrassed apologies for a walk down the street to the lake . It was spring of our junior year in high school, and the evening had the familiar feel of a gentle breeze scented with charcoal and fish. We strolled quietly, our hands clasped.

I broke from his hold, "Race you!" He caught up and nudged me.

"Don't make me pick you up and throw you into the lake," he said.

"Go ahead and try, muscle man!" He strolled toward a long piece of driftwood. I followed. We leaned against the smooth white wood. He cupped sand over my raised knee.

"Lea, where are we going with this?"

"What do you mean?" We had something as real as the breeze moving over the lake.

"I like you a lot. And I want to know how you feel about *us*?" he said.

"I like you a lot, too. I'm glad we're together."

"So, we're taking this seriously, our relationship. Right?"

"Yeah."

We were enjoying the moments: together in high school with friends and family and special occasions made better on account of the other. I hadn't entertained thoughts of a multicultural family, his parents coming to the States, and sharing life with a man that was as different from my family, and especially my father, as I was the same. I was living in the moment. The momentum of falling in love occupied all my energy.

The following Christmas of our senior year, Dima's grandmother visited America. I was excited to meet Grandma and experience a bit of Russia by her. Before she'd arrived, his parents had explained to Dima on the phone that they and Grandma had all applied for visas to visit, but only Grandma's dramatic plea had won over the authorities. "I'm old and might never have another chance to visit my grandson," she had said. She was barely sixty when they issued her a visa — much to her dismay.

"I'm not going to America! Not without you, Tatyana. I refuse. Absolutely not." Her mouth was set, eyes closed. "I am too old to travel across the world by myself. And who knows what might happen in America. No, Russia is my *home*." Viktor paced the living room.

"Mom, you have to go. It's our only chance to see Dimka. A person does not know what she wants until she has it. Once you are in America, you will like it," Tatyana said. We all should have listened more carefully to Grandma.

Grandma arrived at the Holmeses' shortly before their holiday open house. Dima carried her suitcase to his room. It remained a tight bundle from which she pulled what was needed, looking over her shoulder when her back was to the door. She slept with her visa in her bloomers, her money in her bra, and was rigid about keeping them on her at all times.

The first night she was there, her arm laced Dima's as she cried, "Please, gather the family. I have gifts." We circled her in the yellow kitchen as she tried to form words through violent weeping. Her underbite quivered, silver gray head slightly nodded. Dima translated. "Our family loves you. You have given Dima more than we can ever repay. And for this, eternal gratefulness," she bowed. "We wish you health and happiness. We wish you blessings and long life." She hiked her purple housedress up and pulled a silver spoon from her stockings. "A Povozhaev family heirloom, the spoon has been passed from generation to generation three times now. We would like you to accept it as a gift from our family to yours." I handed her a tissue as Susan accepted the spoon, kissed Grandma's wet cheek, and loudly thanked her.

Dima's Russianness became tangible through Grandma: her buttery eggs and fish soups, her strong scent and stubborn pride; her quiet, love, and difference. Dima seemed to think it was all quite natural, at least in the beginning. For two and a half weeks, being with Grandma was like a field trip through Dima's past. There were photo albums, endless stories sometimes translated, and silent hours shared in the hum of the Holmeses' TV.

Dima wanted me at the Holmeses' more often than usual. "You just don't want to hang out with me and Grandma," he said on the phone one Saturday afternoon.

"It's not that. I'm going shopping for a formal dress. They're on clearance at Dillard's."

"Why don't you stop over on your way home from the mall, it's on the way?"

"I'll try." But Grandma slowed things down to a crawl, and I wasn't patient enough to understand. How long could we smile without talking? How much could I eat before tapping my foot, twisting my wristwatch? I added, "But you're coming over for my birthday tonight —" I was nineteen.

Dima drove Grandma twenty minutes from the Holmeses' to my parents' in Susan's red convertible, the wind pushing fiercely against the black leather top that we had had down only months ago on the way to summer parties. I sat like a large doll on Grandma's lap, conscious of my small body against her soft bosom, the feel of her thin cotton pants under my legs. We ate spaghetti as my family began the inquisition.

"Dima, ask her how she likes America," my mother said, smiling at Grandma.

"She likes it, but it is very different from Russia."

"Does she like the food?" Melanie asked.

"Yeah. The food's all right. The people are a lot different. It's very difficult for her to adjust because she's an older person. She's used to the life she has back home." Little of this could be adequately explained over meatballs and garlic bread in the short time with Grandma at my parents'. It was a world of difference just beginning to emerge, and we were all simultaneously quieted and provoked by it.

I imagine Grandma felt trapped. There was laughter and vigorous head nodding as we sat around a polished table with matching dishes. There was a crocheted magnet, J-E-S-U-S, and other religious symbols that were unlike the icons she had in her apartment. Her large body hid under my slight frame with her whispered, "Pozhaluista," rippling against my neck as she reached for the butter. Her arms pressed my sides as she slathered the spaghetti with butter instead of sauce.

Grandma locked herself in her bedroom at the Holmeses' holiday open house, refusing to see anybody but Dima and me. "Come on, Grandma. Just come down and get a plate of food at least. There aren't that many people. Everyone's friendly, I promise," Dima said. We huddled outside the room, listening as she shuffled from the bed and unlocked the door. Thick eyeglasses clouded her swollen face. She slumped into the small rocking chair in the corner, breathing heavily. I stooped down to hug her.

"It's okay. It's okay," I said.

"I feel like a spectacle. Everyone stares at me like I'm an animal in a cage. I can't go down there. I can't do this." Grandma wept into Dima's flannel shirt. We brought her finger foods on a china dish and told Mrs. Holmes she wasn't feeling well and wanted to go home.

Susan changed Grandma's flight so she could leave two weeks earlier.

Grandma was here for Christmas, and the gifts left her sick with regret. She sat on the edge of the bed in her striped cotton pants and gray sweater, bags tightly packed. "Susan told me I could work off my gifts," her eyes widened, "I'll never leave the States!"

"She was only joking, Grandma. Really, she wouldn't make you work—I promise." She wouldn't listen to Dima. She couldn't understand why people would give her things without compensation. Soviet mentality fossilized the belief that nothing was free, including American goodwill. At five, Grandma had nearly died of starvation, and it seemed desperation never left her spirit. During WWII, her family had been starving when her uncle returned home and gave them a crust of bread. As a small girl, Grandma didn't understand why her uncle wouldn't give them more food. She ran after him, begging for more bread. Later, she realized that he hadn't given them any more for fear they'd eat too much, too quickly, and die. She'd never lose a subtle hunger that kept her careful to save and weary of too much at once.

When Grandma left, it was a sort of sad relief, a quick and easy shift from the responsibilities of Russian family. Dima squeezed my hand as soon as we turned our backs from Cleveland's airport, Grandma safely on her way home. "You know what Grandma told me?" he said.

"What?" I yawned.

"She made me promise to marry for love." He stared ahead at the busy road.

Before I left for Malone College and Dima for the University of Findlay, I was at the Holmeses' for steak and asparagus. Jerry shared stories of his trip to St. Petersburg and meeting Dima's parents the first year he was in the States.

"I had to urinate in a Coke bottle! What else could I do? I was stuck on the train! The bodyguards had cautioned me not to leave my room until the train stopped in St. Petersburg and they came for me. I could have been pick pocketed, or worse." A nervous smile played on my face. "No, I'm serious," he said. I nodded. "Oh, this is really amazing, listen to this. I was in the city late one night after dinner, making my way back to the hotel. There were some men huddled behind a car. It was dark. I couldn't make out exactly what was going on. But I swear it looked like they were loading a body bag into the trunk!" He speared his asparagus. I wondered what in the world Russia might be like.

## CHAPTER FIVE

# Spreading Out

At Malone College's orientation, students covered the lawn at sunset. A cross loomed at the top of the chapel just beyond. The campus was beautiful, and I was hopeful. As time passed, however, it seemed some things were limiting.

I didn't feel comfortable when there were open hours to mill around the small campus, to hang out and watch the soccer games, to go shopping with girlfriends. I had tried these things but always longed for my family and Dima. I had expected more comfortable closeness with fellow Christians at Malone. It hadn't made sense to keep such distance, yet this was how my father often handled relationships. In fact, it seemed one reason he and Mom left churches. I didn't want to repeat his tendency with people, but the truth was, sometimes people at Malone made me weary. I was often keenly aware that I did not fit the clean white image so many there portrayed. It could feel as though many were creating an image of "perfect person," but not necessarily Christian, and that the homogeneity stifled a fuller expression of life in Christ. I wondered what it was to be in Christ beyond an image. I sought spiritual depth, which I tried to find at Malone.

"Jesus Freaks" (as they branded themselves in black letters sprawling bright T-shirts, untucked over khaki cutoffs) strolled the campus, some with acoustic guitars under their arms. I hadn't wanted to wear the T-shirts or the new bracelets that said "What would Jesus do?" I didn't wear my hair in braids or pigtails, nor did I sport jean overalls, also en vogue in the late nineties at Malone. I sometimes blamed Dima. Though he didn't say so, I thought he thought the culture odd. There were times when something deeper seemed misguided.

We gathered in the barn, Malone's central meeting hall, about a young black preacher. "Close your eyes and feel the Spirit move!" he bellowed. My eyes almost closed as he approached but I resisted. The smell of sweat and the whine of the microphone was over me as his hand landed on my shoulder. "The spirits of evil will leave you!" As he moved away, I walked past a card table with punch and cookies and out into the evening.

Other times, I was swept away by the blond boy who led praise and worship on Thursday evenings. He strummed the guitar and softly sang about Jesus. He paused to pray with a southern accent, more expressive than my father's prayers had ever been. He never spoke for all, but stayed particular and personal. I always sensed he was sincerely crying out to the Lord as he confessed his pride, vanity, and shame. He asked Jesus to free him by grace, and I silently prayed the same.

When a representative from the Council for Christian Colleges and Universities came to Malone fall semester my sophomore year of college and offered the opportunity to study abroad, I was eager to apply. Our professor was the only black man I had seen on campus (aside from guest preachers) with a boxer's stocky build and evangelist's smile. "I'll just move on out of the way," he said, teeth glowing through a smile. He slipped to the corner of the room, opening his briefcase to appear busy. The woman's thin hands fixed on a stack of brochures.

"We have study programs for Australia, China, Latin America, the Middle East, Oxford, Uganda, and Russia. The programs are funded through tuition costs of students' home colleges and universities. The university you attend abroad then becomes your extension campus. Most students bring spending money, but, depending on where you go, the cost of living is likely much less than in the States."

I would earn the spending cash waiting tables at Red Lobster over Christmas break. My father would think travels abroad a wise investment. He and I had begun to share late night talks on my frequent gallivants back home. He seemed proud of me for attending college and fostering personal faith in Jesus. We talked about the deeper things in life that I didn't as often share with Mom. But he was always asking me why they paid room and board at Malone when I came home so often. Though I spent alternating weekends in Findlay, my father was right — I didn't want to live at Malone.

My professor stood in the corner of the classroom and closed his briefcase. I wondered how Dima would react. Leaving class with the brochure, I read, "A riddle wrapped in a mystery inside an enigma. You must breathe in the incense that hangs in the air of every Orthodox church. Experience the eeriness of Lenin's tomb. Savor rich, creamy borsht. Feel the rumble of Moscow's subway trains." I pinched the edge of the leaflet. The Russian Studies Program was sponsored by the Council for Christian Colleges & Universities and academically grounded in a Christian liberal arts context. The program was a fifteen week study in religion, culture, politics, and economics. The group would stay in Moscow, Nizhny Novgorod, and finally St. Petersburg, with brief excursions to other cities.

I hoped to go. Dima and I had always shared a long distanced relationship, though separate schools was nothing compared to eight thousand miles and an ocean. I worried about exercise and food. I could jump rope, instead of jog. Eat grapefruit, instead of salad. Become a temporary vegetarian, if the meat was unbearable. I wondered how young people lived there and how I might. My greatest concern was learning the Russian language and speaking with his parents. Beyond any care was a naïve thrill to experience Russia and Dima's parents for the first time.

At the University of Findlay, Dima's life began to move beyond hockey. He couldn't travel across the country playing varsity hockey without sacrificing long weekends, which meant our time together and his studies. He chose to play on the club team his first year and continued as their goalie throughout four years at the university.

He met a boy from Moscow also attending Findlay. They were compatible the way he and I were — Dima reserved and calm, his friend expressive and easily excited. Russian and English interlaced their conversations. I often heard 'dude' and 'man' along with a firing of sharp sounds: "Shto ty delaesh, dude?!" They played video games, watched slapstick comedy (Russian and American). Their common past became a touchstone that seemed both a source of pride and determination. They wanted to become successful in America and contrived plans such as buying potato peelers in bulk for their parents to sell back home, translating for Russian immigrants, or opening a Russian restaurant.

Findlay was a refreshing break from Malone. The disheveled way of life was exciting. We talked about religion, politics, and culture, considering the world beyond the U.S. Dima's friend's family was Christian and Muslim, and I began to wonder about other faiths, like Islam, and the people and places where such beliefs were as important to others as Christianity was to me. At the Moscow boy's apartment, we drank room temperature soda from chipped mugs. We ate "breakfasts" of fried dough and cabbage in the afternoons. We returned from parties late at night, making sandwiches with generic Myers' bread and slices of meat left on a greasy dish.

When Dima's friend's mother came, she stayed with her son in the apartment for at least a month. She kept the beds made and rinsed dishes. Their home smelled of cabbage and oil, and she sprayed deodorizers throughout the tall rooms. It wasn't long before she called Dima 'son' and me 'daughter.' While being Russian bonded them, Dima's friend and his family were exceptionally loving and friendly. Our closeness, despite our differences — or maybe in part because of them and the ensuing interest — contrasted with the distant friendships I had at Malone.

Dima spent full days and nights with his friend. The mother would greet me with a kiss, sausage on her breath, a throaty chuckle emanating from deep inside her. She was an attractive woman with dark Uzbek skin and eyes. She learned English from watching T.V. and baked tortes, drizzled with condensed milk and caramel, to sell at the small store around the corner. She seemed very willing to embrace America, as she often squeezed me tightly in her small, strong arms. "I luv yoo," she would flash a gold-toothed smile. The mother sighed often, shaking her head and mumbling "life difficult," an expression she knew in English. I'd smile meekly and agree. Sometimes we strolled to the store, and she'd link her arm through mine as we ambled slowly through town for milk and hotdogs. She'd peruse the nearly spoiled produce on clearance and usually leave with something she'd turn delicious.

She repeatedly told me, "Dima good boy," a possessive smile folding into her soft cheeks. He became serious about school and began courses in International Business and Marketing. It seemed to his advantage that he was a foreigner, and fairly Americanized, as his professors took interest in him. One time at a local bar where Dima's Russian friend worked, his composition instructor hung out with us, sipping beer through a straw. She appeared an aged hippy, wispy hair draping a round shoulder, plain face full on Dima. With her back to me, my eyes roamed the flower pattern curling the thin cotton. The bar was dim and a votive candle floated in a glass bowl beside a jar of biscotti. I took a chocolate cookie, smiling at Dima's Russian friend as he paused from wiping the glass bottle of rum. The instructor's sandaled foot was still and made me conscious of my own tapping against the barstool.

Dima and his Russian friend attended Findlay's International Fair, for which they prepared a Russian beet salad — Dima mixing and chopping, his buddy laughing and talking. Dima wore a leather vest, given by a rich boy from Jordan, over a pale green button down to the International Fair. Students from India, China, Latin America, and the Middle East offered dishes of their homeland's traditional foods. The aroma and languages of particular lands floated together. I stood behind the "Russia" sign scooping the bright beet salad onto plates. Heavy spices and heat settled as thin oil on our skin.

On the way back to the apartment, I whispered to Dima to have his friend stop at Myer's Grocery for carrots and Ranch dressing. "We're ordering pizza. Why do you need carrots?" But at this early stage in our relationship, my peculiarities hadn't seemed to bother him, at least not to the point of refusing me. I tickled his forearm.

"Dude, Lea needs vegetables." They chuckled.

Dima changed into his tie dye and cutoffs while his buddy ordered pizza, and I felt glad to be among Americanized Russians, to be 'home.' While I dipped their crusts and my carrots in Ranch and read, they played video games long into the night.

One of Dima's hockey teammates loaned us his car for emergency visits. Oftentimes, I shared a ride with peers from Malone who lived in Findlay and left for home on the weekends. When there seemed no other way to be together, he chanced it with the car. It was a Nova from the eighties, aged yellowish white, the bottom ravaged by rust. As long as the heat was on high, Dima said the engine shouldn't overheat (even though the gauge indicated it was severely overheated). We couldn't open the doors from the outside without particular jiggling and the interior smelled slightly like manure, we guessed from years of transporting hockey equipment. We saved our money for a Toyota Corolla.

Dima rumbled into Malone's parking lot, and I ran out to see him, nestling into his neck and Dove soap. Entering into Malone's culture with him was a precarious event at best. In the beginning, I'd taken him to "celebration" in the barn. At celebration, we sang and clapped with an hour of contemporary Christian praise and worship songs. Then, a small sermon was delivered by one of the student band members. Dima stood statuesque among the rest of us clapping and singing.

"I don't know what you expect me to do," he said.

"I try in all the strange situations you put me in," I argued. He didn't argue back, but said he was sorry in usual calm. I leaned into his warm body.

While in Findlay one weekend, Dima and his Russian friend and I went to a party, talking on a porch under the stars. Laughter and Rusted Root pulsated from the rickety house. Dima's friend asked about the turquoise cross draping my collar. "What do you believe?" I asked him. He said he was Muslim but wondered about the differences between our faiths. Each one was on a personal journey, and getting to know people from other countries helped me see the universal, mutual need we shared. There was only one Lord Jesus Christ, and with everything in me I longed to know Him more — and to share faith in Him with others.

"It's the same God," he said, looking up at the stars. God was God. That we might know Him was overwhelming and necessary.

**CHAPTER SIX**

# Going into Russia

We were home for Christmas and went swimming in the Holmeses' indoor pool. Dima sat on the steps in the shallow end where a pool light glowed warmly behind him. I swam laps, moving to his end of the pool and opening my eyes under the water to reach for his leg. I emerged from the water and slipped between his legs. His swimming shorts floated up his long thighs and billowed over my hands. I leaned down to study faint lines on his upper thighs, asking what the scars were from. He turned his thigh and said he had stretch marks from the nine inches he'd grown his first year in the States.

I slipped under the water again and opened my eyes. I floated, palms on his knees, and looked at his pale legs glowing from the light behind him. Somersaulting from him, I swam laps.

Growing up, most things felt were expressed. Whether tearful hugs of apology, or tickle attacks in the backseat of the minivan with my sister, growing up was loud. Once, when I was a child, we drove to South Carolina in an old Nova and rented a one room cabin steps from the ocean. We lived on Mom's bran muffins for the week. We batted horseflies swarming above my grandmother's quilt, a rich swill of colors, which we'd used through the years as the beach blanket. One evening walking along the beach, my father cried, "I've got a stingray! Diane?" We followed my mother as my father dragged the writhing animal to the edge of the water. Its gray back glistened with the lingering energy of the day. My sister giggled, her toe dangerously near the flapping tail. Our father said we had to keep it away from the shore. He'd talked to other fishermen who said a stingray had stung a child. So we stood there, watching the animal move less and less until it lay deflated in the sand. My father's arms flexed while he carried it in a towel to a private corner of the beach. My mother dug a shallow hole with my plastic shovel from McDonald's, and Dad gently placed the stingray in. We scooped sand over it.

I stopped swimming in the Holmeses' pool at the opposite end from Dima. My parents' control of situations taught me to fight nature instead of working with it, to hurry to resolution instead of waiting, to protect myself, sometimes at the cost of others. We could have waited till the next day to see if the stingray might have gone deeper into the ocean. We could have moved further down the beach. On the other hand, Dima's parents weren't as quick to make a situation come together safely and efficiently. In letting Dima come to the States, their lives were conditioned to wait on variables they had little control over.

I shouted, "Hey, stallion, are you planning to just sit there like a lump all night?" He dove under the water and raced towards me.

We returned to school after break and to the news of acceptance into the Russian Studies Program. I called Dima. "Are you there? Honey?"

"Lea, Lea calm down. I'm happy. This is good news. Really good news. I've got some pictures and stuff for you to take to my parents. I can't believe you're going to see them." His voice was even, reined in.

As nineteen American students from various Protestant colleges and universities boarded our flight into Moscow, I was in the moment and calm. More than ever before, I felt God's presence as the plane took off. By the time we landed, it was night in Russia. The Sheremet'evo International Airport had almost five-hundred Western-styled hotel rooms, complete with amenities one expected in America: swimming pool and sauna, fitness and massage centers, fine dining (including Coca-Cola) and toilet seats. The airport was not as foreign as I had imagined. Many of the signs were in English and Russian. One advertised a souvenir shop in the "V.I.P. Lounge." The pitch read: "Escape the ordinary and come shopping in Canada." How strange to think Russian dolls, perfumes, and travel maps ordinary.

We walked towards our program director Henry. He was a smaller man in a wool coat. He wore dark shoes and pants, a Russian fur hat in hand. His face was smooth and pale below a sparse combover. His eyes had a look of gentle concentration and he appeared exhausted or sad. He waved his hand for the group to follow. One of our program handouts provided background information explaining that he had lived twenty years in Russia during which time he had worked for the Coalition of Christian Colleges and Universities, touring groups of students through the Russian Studies Program. During summer vacations, he often returned to his hometown in Kansas.

After moving quickly through passport and visa checks, the group followed Henry, passing militiamen leaning against a smudged wall and laughing. Henry pointed ahead to the Bureau de Change Facility. "You'll need to convert your currency," he began in a soft tone. He turned to the guards and spoke in Russian. I finally felt I was in another country.

"We'll take the express to Ismailovo Hotel," he stretched his thin voice over the passing militia. Unlike in the States, Russian people didn't smile at passersby. At first, I thought the people were rude and didn't talk much. An elderly woman had strategically set goods in front of the exit from the airport. She nodded to the Russian dolls, jewelry, and maps displayed on a metal table. "Buy?" she said, her papery face breaking with a toothless grin. We milled about her goods and spent freely.

Bitter wind was against my cheeks as the group loaded the bus to Ismailovo Hotel. The driver swayed to a melancholic American pop song from the fifties. A smile held at the edge of his dark eyes. He was the first Russian to smile at us. His face was worn. Miniature international flags hung above the front window with the USA flag in the middle. As the bus rumbled through night, a yellow light glowed under the flags: Afghanistan, Australia, Belarus, Canada, Chile, China, Croatia, Czech Republic, Israel. Henry wrestled duffle bags from the bus, and the driver tossed our luggage to us.

"Go on to the hotel!" Henry motioning us across the street above the din of speeding cars and hollering taxi drivers. I bit the inside of my cheek and balanced a bag around my shoulder, purse around my neck, and rolled the suitcase through the slush.

"Trust no one," Dima had said. His words resounded over and over as I struggled through the loud darkness and past the taxis.

"Need some help?" An attractive American peer shouted as an old fashioned car rumbled inches in front of him. Cars sped haphazard and close as the group scattered through the street.

I thanked him and pushed the Student Bible, notebook, and hairbrush deeper into my carryon with shaking hands. I offered him the suitcase as honks and sharp words shot through gasoline and exhaust. Russia seemed less a romantic mystery and more an action packed thriller as I tore through the slush.

Newness and hope filled me as I lay in a small bed in a Moscow hotel. Through a large window, the gray city was still and smoke billowed from factories. High rise apartments appeared dank shades of cold and contrasted with the cozy room, one of two thousand in the massive hotel. Unlike Russian apartments set with small tables and tea sets and draped by warm rugs, the hotel had been renovated the year before. The place had the feel of a tidy, basic hotel in the States — other than the black ceramic tub and the complicated bedding. The sheets were brightly patterned and covered by a floral spread encased in a sort of large pillowcase. A square, removed from the center, revealed the top blanket. It was considered unsanitary in Russia for the blanket to be kept outside the protective bed cover, which seemed ironically fussy.

The world outside the hotel was striking. In the course of ten days that followed, we strolled Red Square and snapped photographs of a bride and groom standing before the Cathedral of St. Basil. "This church was built to commemorate Ivan the Terrible's conquest of Kazan in 1551. St. Basil was a Holy Fool, from that beautiful Russian tradition of asceticism and piety," Henry began. The sun was bright, the sky as blue as an onion dome behind the bride. I was floating above myself and anything seemed possible.

Once in the center of the Kremlin, Henry motioned around the six buildings, including three enormous cathedrals. "If the heart of Russia is the Kremlin, then its soul is the oldest area within the Kremlin, Cathedral Square, the so called 'City of God,'" he said. I felt miniscule at the center of the massive architecture, at once understanding why Dima thought churches in the West didn't look like "houses of God."

There was a massive limestone Cathedral of the Assumption with icons below five proportioned gilt domes with Orthodox crosses. "For centuries, this church served as the central cathedral of Russia and the place where czars were crowned," Henry spoke softly. The church looked stern, less ornate than the other cathedrals inside the Kremlin. As we stepped inside, Henry explained, "The church was designed by Italian Aristotle Fioravante, but in the style of traditional Russian architecture from ancient cities."

The group was quiet once inside the first of many Orthodox cathedrals. Figures of saints and martyrs sprawled pillars, window jambs, and reinforcing arches. There were depictions of Jesus Christ and Mary as well as ancient scenes from the Bible.

"The Bolshevik Government transferred to Moscow in 1918, and for the next seven decades the church was closed. Rumor had it that Stalin allowed an Easter service at the Cathedral of the Assumption in 1941 to pray for the country's salvation when the Nazis were fast approaching," Henry said. His eyes lifted to the upper tiers of the north and south walls where scenes from Mary's life were painted.

Had she doubted the angels when they told her she would give birth to Christ, though she was a virgin? She'd responded as God's servant, completely obedient to His will, though she could have feared in misunderstanding. I wondered how earlier years had prepared her for such trusting and how seeing an angel would elicit my own faith. What would Joseph have made of her confession of miraculous conception of Christ? It seemed unbelievable that faith could allow belief in a reality so unnatural.

The attractive peer stood in front of me in a fluffy Columbia jacket and snapped a picture of the Apocalypse fresco on the west wall. Saints flanked Christ and sinners mourned beneath Him in hell — response to His uncreated light torture or bliss. The faces in the icons were similarly proportioned with wide-set eyes, long noses, delicately closed mouths. Light and dark spread through the scenes like the wrestling of good and evil on earth. The boy's bright hat bobbed in front of me as he snapped photos. At first glance, we may have seemed out of place among the ancient work, but underneath the bright colors and modern styles how different were we from ancient people? We chose to follow Christ or oppose Him and to likewise cooperate with the mystical reality.

"Much of this dates back to the seventeenth century," Henry explained pointing to twelve gilt bronze chandeliers and several multi-tiered candelabra overhead. I couldn't imagine people in 1999 worshipping among such antiquity.

As we toured the "City of God," the Cathedral of Christ the Savior was being rebuilt. "By 1931, Stalin destroyed the church with plans to remake the building into a palace of Soviets. Atop the remade building, larger than the Empire State Building, he intended to resurrect a colossal statue of Lenin. After several attempts to construct and stabilize the foundations, frustrated by the shifting earth from the Moscow River, the construction was abandoned and replaced by a public swimming pool," Henry said. Worship could be redirected, but it was impossible to quench the human need to worship.

We slowly moved from the center of the Kremlin, and Henry told us it was a symbol of Russia and the oldest part of the city. It was easy to recognize the importance people here placed on grandeur. An enormous chipped bell, the largest in the world at two-hundred tons, and a forty-ton cannon, were both created in the sixteenth century for the tsar, and neither had ever been used.

After a week and a half in Moscow, we visited a circus one evening. I looked forward to the change of pace from countless churches and museums. We bought buttery popcorn and ice cream bars and slipped into the bleachers. We snapped pictures as acrobats mounted in a human pyramid. The place was red: carpet oval below the bleachers, walls, trampoline, and bow ties around tigers' necks. The energy was dizzying.

We continued on excursions. In Russia, the churches, museums, even the circus seemed similarly more extreme. I thought about Dima and how he wouldn't take vitamins, calling them 'pills,' but would drink honey and garlic in steaming whole milk because it was natural. It began to make more sense to me after spending time in Russia. Nature seemed closer to people and their responses with it amazing.

Russian art was beautiful. The rich, soul-wrenching chants of the Church; the enormous grandeur of the buildings, especially the churches, cave-like and majestic at once; the somber melodies of folk songs, weaving a land and people back through centuries of mystery and heartache, celebration and mourning — the culture was marvelously flamboyant and beautiful. I felt love for Russia. God was present, and the dominant feeling was joy.

I branched off from the group as we explored the Tretiakov Gallery of Fine Art and stood before the "Vladimir Icon of the Mother of God." Somber colors depicted Christ's mother holding Him in her right arm, her head bowed to His cheek, His arm around her neck. Her left hand reached up to the Child, showing all the way to God. The painting was tender and though I'd never experienced icons or the Mother of God before, it felt familiar somehow. The salvation of the world began with her faith. A mother's love emerged as an illustration to me of the love of God. It could seem hard to believe that God continued to love His creation even as it often denied Him. Yet, like my mother, He would remain patient and steadfast.

The Mother of God seemed fiercely feeling but also reserved. With an ache behind my chest, I felt her affection was deep and somehow beyond human expression. I had never prayed to Mary, but my soul responded in those stilling moments. According to Orthodox Church history, a Russian prince took the icon of the Mother of God to Vladimir where miracles began to happen. At the time, Tatars threatened Moscow, and with hopes to pray protection over the city, the icon was placed in a cathedral in the Moscow Kremlin. The enemy retreated. In another account of a miracle from the icon, the Mother of God appeared to some in dreams. The icon wept myrrh and healed and protected people who prayed to her.

At a small kiosk, I bought a CD of the "All Night Service to the Vladimir Icon of the Mother of God,"[1] sung by the choir of a St. Nicholas Church in Tolmachi. The icon on the cover drew me. While I hadn't considered praying to anyone but Jesus, like all loving mothers who need not be asked to pray for a child, it was possible the Mother of God's entreaties to her Son encouraged an opening of my spirit.

Though we were within walking distance of the Novodevichii Convent, Pomorskaya Old Believers Commune, and the Cathedral of the Annunciation, the group didn't go to these churches to worship. Instead, we gathered in Henry's hotel room for praise and worship and to make plans for the day. His room was uncomfortably warm, heated by hot water pipes common to most older buildings in Russia. The group harmonized in pop Christian songs as a boy with glasses strummed an acoustic guitar, tapping his foot on the hotel comforter. We passed dried fruit and chocolate and bowed our heads to pray for Russia: presidential elections, tension with Chechnya, and the new market economy. We prayed for peace at home with President Clinton. When we left for Russia, there had been talk of impeachment over the President's affair with Monica Lewinsky.

We had been in Moscow almost six days and the group wouldn't travel to St. Petersburg until the end of the trip. Dima's father boarded the train for an overnight trip to meet me. The night before we met, I wrestled the blanket out of the complicated folds and leaned a stiff back against the sheets. The alarm was set for seven, an hour and a half before Viktor was supposed to arrive. I thought of Dima — his quiet, shoulder bobbing laugh, his gentle hands and calming way. I couldn't sleep and my stomach was a knot. The toilet in our room was out of order. The phone rang before six-thirty.

"Hello?"

"Leeeea. It's me, Veeektor. Ah, get Henry." I pulled a sweater from my bag and stepped into the jeans I'd worn all week. I knocked over

---

[1] Alexei Pouzakov, conductor, (St. Nicholas Church, November 1996).

the brush, picked it up and moved it through my hair, and ran down the hall to get Henry.

"I'm sorry to wake you. Ah — Dima's father's here. I need you to translate."

"Just a minute." He soon emerged with a meek smile, smelling like grapefruit, and briskly led the way to the cafeteria. The dining hall was empty but for the workers, and music played softly as ladies rolled buffet carts: hotdogs, cups of thin yogurt, dumplings, and fruit. A small Christmas tree wedged in the corner of the room, and ornaments hung from the ceiling. Unlike in the States, there were no bright and smiling Santa Clauses, Christmas tree napkins, or spice cakes at the buffet. The holiday seemed downsized in Russia, hardly noticeable once people filed into the bright cafeteria.

A full-bodied man with a shadowy face approached us. "Ztrastvtya," Viktor said and shook Henry's hand. In a flash, heavy arms engulfed me like a giant inner tube. My cheek pressed his cold sweat. At the table, Viktor's narrow lips rested in a half smile and the corner of his mouth twitched. Soft lines splintered at the corners of his eyes. He had Dima's triangular nose and full eyebrows, but an extra sixty pounds blanketed his father's smaller frame. He spoke with his eyes on me as Henry began to translate.

"Viktor asks about your family."

"My family is well. They're nervous I'm here for the semester," I laughed. "But they know how much I wanted to see Russia." I straightened my back against the chair, smiled self consciously into Viktor's weary eyes. It was difficult to understand Viktor's emotion. I nodded, inched to the edge of the seat, but seemed unable to move the conversation along.

"How is Dima?" He began speaking to Henry before I responded. Henry appeared skeptical, and Viktor's words were left untranslated. I said Dima would be calling and sends his love, walking to a large metal pot of tea and filling three cups. Returning with tea, I listened as "Putin" and "Yeltsin" popped in their conversation. The following year, 2000, would mark Russian history as the first transfer of power from one leader to the next by a constitution. Some citizens were hopeful. Yeltsin's passing of the presidential torch to Putin without a revolution, and the new President's promise of fewer taxes, more work, and a stabilized economy encouraged the optimists. However, Putin was young, and others, such as Dima's parents, doubted a man they had not heard of one year ago.

"Dima's father wonders if the people were better off under communism. They had food coupons then. Now, the people work harder and harder, hoping for their pay. Sometimes it comes after three months." Viktor interrupted, and Henry nodded. "He wants me to tell you that if you were a teacher in Russia right now, you would only make twelve dollars a month. Not enough to live on with the cost of inflation. He thinks this is why the average worker is turning corrupt." Henry said Dima's parents' perception was common for the average worker caught between two worlds. In one, the government provided everything. In the other, the government provided next to nothing.

Viktor patted the sweat dampened T-shirt between his unzipped jacket flaps. He looked into the distance as Henry said, "He wants to be sure you're safe. Wear your money under your clothing." It was almost frightening how little confidence Dima's father appeared to have in his country.

"Viktor, ah, I will learn po-russky yazik soon." His face was straight, eyes far off. Did he hear me? Understand?

"Leea, I ahh, kak po-anglisky yazik? I call skoro. Ya budu robotat." He was slow to speak, seemingly rolling thoughts and words through his mind, and painfully slow to leave. I forced myself not to look down at the watch.

Henry returned with his plate of food. Viktor spoke to Henry in Russian while he lifted a cup of plain kafir to his slight lips. Viktor slowly raised from the table and looked down at me. We had shared less than a half hour, and I was moved at the great distance Viktor had covered for our meeting that morning, though he had to return for his bus route early the next morning. I stood, and he circled to my side of the table. I linked my arm through his puffy jacket. He stood straight, feet together as if in military attention, and smiled down at me. We walked to the entrance of the cafeteria. He wrapped me in his arms, "I luv you, Leea," he said in deliberate strokes of English.

"I love you, too, Viktor." I found it hard to believe he had ever been brusque. Back at the table, Henry asked if Dima and I were engaged as his father had said. I told him we were not, surprised that he had said so.

It was late afternoon and the group was going to hear an aspiring Evangelical preacher. We gathered in the metro station. A woman just past middle age looked off in the distance while selling tickets behind a booth. I asked for a ticket in Russian. At first, I wondered if she was hard of hearing and spoke up, but she didn't respond even as I reworded the simple phrase. Finally, Henry shimmied to the front of the line and requested twenty metro passes for the group. She nodded and issued the tickets to Henry without delay.

The metro was packed with hardly a space between people. A young man turned and faced me. He spoke in English and asked my name and how I liked Russia. His body odor mixed with the smell of new leather, and he smiled without showing his teeth. He asked what I was doing that evening, and I nervously laughed and said I was busy with the group. He slipped a scrap of paper in my hand with a telephone number and his name written in Russian and English. He grinned and filed off the bus. The paper fluttered from my fingers.

We walked a brisk mile to a plain building. We descended a steep stairwell to an unfinished basement with orange chairs. "Make selves at home please," a young blond man spoke with a microphone on a makeshift stage. He wore jeans and a sweatshirt and carried a Bible. Less than a handful of Russians sat on the other side of the room.

"This is Andrei," Henry said on the stage with a microphone. "He is training to be an Evangelical preacher," a whistle came from the crowd. Henry smiled. "He is going to share a sermon with us and afterward lead us in praise and worship." There was applause. The preacher's accent was rich and mixed with Russian. He seemed nervous as he paced the stage with an occasional stomp of his foot to bring home a point. I tried to follow him, then to imagine what he might be saying.

I excused myself for the restroom and ambled through a long hallway that reminded me of an empty high school. A yellowish light came from behind me, but the hallway was otherwise dim. The walls were smooth stone with hot water pipes. I marveled at the surreal calm that filled me. I shivered and slowly moved to the end of the hall. There was no pressing desire to see Andrei preach. It was important that Christianity spread through Russia, but what I saw with Andrei made me feel closed to what seemed fake and forced. I didn't think there needed to be grandeur to express holiness. The icons and gold of the Orthodox churches had seemingly turned places of worship into museums. I doubted people could focus on personal relationships with Jesus Christ in the distraction of it all. Yet, Andrei's approach didn't seem right either. What was authentic Christianity, and how might it be far reaching and universal?

Some Russians resisted Western Christianity just as some in the West, including many in our group, didn't perceive Eastern Christianity as the way to God. What was the beginning point to faith beyond culture? If even the demons believed and trembled, then being Christian was more than merely belief. It seemed about living in Christ — which was more than understanding in my head and feeling love in my heart. While being Christian certainly included thinking and feeling, it was what I did with what developed internally that seemed to matter more than I'd realized before. What was the way to fuller life in Christ? I felt weak hugging a warm water pipe on the floor and asked God for protection and guidance. I asked to learn what He had for me to know. I felt absolutely held, and it was the Mother of God who held me.

That evening, the group gathered once again in Henry's hotel room. We had stopped for dinner at a small store similar to a Western convenience shop. Pear nectar, smoked sausage, dense, slightly sweet cookies, and a jar of cheap caviar with rolls. I sat cross legged on the hotel bed slowly chewing a poppyseed roll. Henry began, "It is imperative that we support the Evangelical Movement in Russia now. Otherwise, these young Russians won't survive in a predominantly Orthodox country."

Just before settling in Nizhny Novgorod for the twelve week routine at the university, we visited the Golden Ring, a circle of ancient Russian towns situated to the northwest of Moscow. Henry spoke above the din of the group engaged in breakfast. He told us we would see ancient Russian architecture of the twelfth through seventeenth centuries at cathedrals in Suzdal and Vladimir.

The breakfast table was animated with conversation. In general, the group seemed to be loosening up. Physical discomforts had intimately revealed us to one another. One girl suffered with a desperate yeast infection, which she had tried to heal with strawberry kafir (yogurt). Monistat was flown in. Many of us were caught between a rock and a way too soft place — keeled over cement holes in bowel irritation. We talked: was it the foreign cheeses, the beet and cabbage soups, the "unsafe" water we used to brush our teeth? We joked about getting fat on the Russian diet, about wearing our pajamas to the theatre, and about the impossible language. At this stage, we were light and such matters were more entertaining than bothersome. It was early.

We loaded a bus with gray upholstered seats and green carpet to travel to the Golden Ring. It was clean and roomy, not unlike a new Greyhound in the States. Henry spoke at the front of the bus, "The Golden Ring has become a tourist route in the northeastern part of what used to be the State of Muscovy."

"By the 1950s, much of Russian architecture was in danger of complete disintegration, but many of the buildings were restored after World War II," Henry's voice was a mix of pride and sadness. We rode in silence, scribbling postcards home, ferreting through bags for music or photo albums. I borrowed a CD player and lifted my knees to the back of the seat in front of me, closing my eyes as Orthodox Church music rolled through the headphones. Deep comfort: heart slowing, shoulders easing. It was possible to crossover, to drift from the rumble of the bus, the soft laugh from someone nearby, even the agitations of the body. It was within me — this gentle lull past all thoughts. It was like sleep, but conscious, as tangible as the swipe of my palm against the cool metal of the seat, and so different from the excitement that often fluttered my heart. Peace was still.

As we continued through churches, my sense of reverence ebbed. There were no worshippers, priests, or choirs. There were no candles or incense. It seemed to me a frozen flavor of Russian asceticism and piety which begged the question: Why was all this architecture, iconography, and ancient tradition necessary to worship the Lord? Why did Christianity vary so as not to be recognizable between the East and the West? Such cultural division made worship appear to be more about a person's time and place than a universal and unchanging God whose one kingdom dwelt within the human soul. Each distinct expression of one's life in His was good and holy. Together in our differences, we were one. Still, there had to be a unifying way of worship that taught Christians how to become more in Christ as we journeyed on. Such a way didn't seem a place but an experience of holiness that was deep and spiritual.

We traipsed through a field without a mark on the snow. Sun glistened in the bitter cold as we made our way to the Church of the Intercession on the Nerl River. At the top of the church was a silver dove. I had the overwhelming urge to pray as faith flowed.

On the outskirts of Suzdal, we ate lunch in a hut with red checkered cloths. Men and women in bright costumes filled teacups and carried baskets of bread to our tables. Ladies began twirling like red and white pinwheels in a folkdance called *barynya* (ladylike). Traditionally, the song and dance was used by simple folk to address ladies of higher class. Skirts swirled, hands clapped, feet stomped. Russian men in the front rows began singing and squatting low to the ground. Some played small stringed instruments like a banjo and tambourine. In the frenzy, I could barely hear myself laughing. Steam rose from bread and stew that sizzled in a clay pot.

## CHAPTER SEVEN

# Walking Deeper

The train into Nizhny Novgorod was a picture of the past with square windows and army green aluminum. Heavy heat filled the hall and small yellow lights lined the ground. I slid my luggage next to a folded blanket and sheet on a lower bunk. Two beds the size and feel of a bench were wedged against the wall. A nightstand with a pinkish light was under a small window. By four in the morning, we arrived in Nizhny to stay for twelve weeks.

Russian students from the Nizhny Novgorod State University met us at the train station and led us to the dormitory. Unlike in the States, few Russian students stayed in the dorms. Instead, they lived in nearby apartments with their families. The sick, elderly, or people without an apartment of their own stayed in the dormitory for months at a time. It seemed more like a shelter in the States than a university's dormitory.

When the group arrived at the entrance of the old Soviet building, a tiny woman with eyeglasses circling half her face smiled. "Boys, here! Move bags here!" She pointed to the tall cement building, shaking her thin face and whispering "kholodna," cold, a word we knew well by then.

"Hello, Henry. Good group here, huh?" They exchanged kisses on the cheek, a common greeting between close ones, and we followed boys in black leather jackets. Once inside a living room area with a TV and dark couches, the woman began official introductions.

"I Vera. Work with Henry many years. Very good man, very good." Her smile reached the bottom of her glasses. "I lead International Program at university. Too bad not summer. Here, Oka and Volga Rivers very beautiful." She sighed and pushed her glasses against her nose. "No problem. International student, Sasha." She nodded to a dark-haired boy with a clear face, broad shoulders, and waist as small as mine. "He show you around. Still much to do, even in winter season." Sasha's smile hinted that he would be our first glimpse of a Russian Romeo.

Henry said, "Nizhny will offer you the experience of the average Russian person." As he spoke, Vera passed out gray sweatshirts with a logo of the city: a red deer in a white field with black horns and hoofs, the city's coat of arms. In Russian, "Nizhny Novgorod State University," sprawled sweatshirts. I touched the letters, sounded out the shapes, and balled it into the corner of my suitcase.

"Go to dorm rooms. Boys help with bags. Any problems and I help. Okay?" She almost smiled, then quickly pivoted to Henry and began speaking in Russian.

The dorm was red with thin carpet and pale walls looming three times as high as my dorm in the States. There were two thin cots on either side of a wide desk, which quickly hosted a smorgasbord of American life in Russia: an English-Russian dictionary and flashcards, a jump rope and rag, bottles of boiled water and grapefruit, and deodorant and sea-mist body spray. There was one closet with a cement ledge and a bent rail to hang clothes. We continued to live out of our suitcases. The room was without windows and veiled late January's descent into February days of "General Winter." Despite three weeks without sunlight, in the dormitory it was warm and bright.

From the start, Nizhny Novgorod felt different than Moscow and the other cities we had toured. As Russia's third largest city and a center of trade and culture, I expected it to be busier. When the hot water shut off, it wasn't turned on sometimes for days. In Henry's apartment, the group shared one computer to email home (fifteen minutes a week) couched between boxes and a single bed. The room had stacks of books, a few blown-glass animals, and Soviet dolls.

A walk down Bolshaya Pokrovskaya Street to Minin Square offered the fullest taste of city life in Nizhny: McDonald's, a closet like film development shop, and a general market stocked with packets of American instant coffee, Russian music, and French perfume. There were gypsies with children from Southern Russia. Sections of the boardwalk were under construction and covered with floorboards but few workers were seen fixing things. The city seemed frozen silent.

As I walked through Nizhny, being in Russia became less a thrill and more a test of endurance. I respected the strength of Russians in surviving as a nation through the course of many years under difficult rulers and in a drastic climate. What's more, they did so with a strong sense of community, ultimately centered on God in the Orthodox Christian Faith.

A digital thermometer across from the university read a temperature below freezing. The cold was less romantic, sometimes even unbearable for the brief periods we had to be out in it. I pushed myself to get serious about the main reasons I was here: to learn some Russian, meet Dima's parents, and experience the culture. Though converting to Orthodoxy wasn't on my list, the Faith was entwined in the culture and I was drawn to it.

We walked to the university on a blank day, and long icicles were suspended from birch trees. I slowed down to blow my nose. A creak sounded through the spindly branches when an icicle fell on my head. I trudged towards the university and into the classroom, rubbing the back of my coat dusted by salt. We had three hours before tea. The class usually began with the teacher leading us in the Russian alphabet and a birthday or folk song. Our language teacher wore a small skirt, a floral shawl wrapping her petite shoulders.

"Leeea, tsk, tsk, tsk," she said with wide eyes, accented by thin brows. I wanted to ask what the problem was, but she scampered out of the room and returned with a dampened handkerchief. "Davay, davay," she motioned for me to give her the coat. I hesitated.

"Nyet, nyet, give Lena. Ya budu," evidently, there was no use telling her I would do it as she cocked her head and tapped herself. She gently reached for the jacket, and there was the scent of lilacs and peppermint. She was in her thirties and beautiful. She had a child but was not married. "I am Mother," she said in English, a cross between a shy smile and pout playing over her full lips. She folded my cleaned coat over the chair, smoothed her skirt and pressed pink lips together before proceeding to the front of the classroom. She picked up a stick and pointed to laminated pictures corresponding with a letter from the alphabet.

The American group was assigned field experiences as part of our coursework while in Nizhny. I spoke with an English class at the Philological Institute. I had worried about what to say, but the strawberry blond teacher pulled me into her "office" (a closet sized storage room) to ask questions about the pronunciation of English words. At once, the atmosphere was curious and inviting. Students wasted no time firing questions in clear English:

"What music do you listen to?"

"What pets do you have?"

"How do young Americans make money?" Some students leaned forward, and no heads were in hands or resting on desks. Some giggled at the strange sounds of rapid American English, as they had been instructed more slowly and with British English. The conversation turned to more serious matters.

"Why do Americans care what President Clinton does in his private life?" a boy asked, waving a lock of hair from his broad forehead. "President's sex life not for public concern, no?" This young man had moments ago led the class in a traditional Russian love song.

"Our culture was founded on Christianity, and many believe our leaders should be moral. We expect our President to be faithful to his wife and to us." The pursuit of happiness was founded on life and liberty that stemmed from faith in God, as the Founding Fathers had known. The pursuit of happiness was in the process of hard work and submission to that which was above and beyond the self. There was moral responsibility, especially for the President, to uphold values and serve the people under God. Even in an increasingly secular country with divided Christianity, it seemed many people still expected an honest and faithful president.

I walked into the evening and took a metro towards Henry's apartment. Once off the bus, I strolled past a snowy field and opened the iron door to the apartment. Warm smells of cabbage and noodles floated in the air, whetting my appetite for the sweets Henry would have bought.

"Come in," Henry said, his thin lips a closed-mouth grin. He turned from the door to the kitchen that smelled of sugar and cinnamon. I untied my boots and slid off my coat. "I'm making bread. Like dates?" Thoughts of my mother's date bread made my mouth water. Bowls of ice cream bars, popcorn, dried apricots, crackers, and nuts spread the kitchen. I filled a plastic plate and joined the group lounging on a braided rug, dark futon, and folding chairs.

"You have a phone call, Lea," Henry said. I shimmied into the computer room.

"Hello?" I hoped it was Dima and feared it was his father, for whom I hadn't prepared a Russian conversation.

"Lea. How are you?" Dima's voice felt like honey in dark tea.

"Okay. I was just thinking about you."

"Oh yeah? What were you thinking?"

"Just how I miss you and this distance apart is really tough."

"I know. But if we survive this, we can survive anything — right?" His voice was always steady, but there was something in the way he said "right" that made me pause. Was he doubting? I needed him to be strong. To believe everything would work out and we'd be together before we knew it.

"You know, we might get married sooner than you think," he said.

"You can't keep a secret to save your life, Dima! You know I'm waiting. Your dad seems to think I am your fiancée —"

"Hey, I told him he could call you that. That's okay, right?" I laughed over Henry's concerns about Dima being Russian, but he skipped over that and asked if I was careful, echoing his father's cautions. I assured him there was nothing to worry about. Neil Young's "Like a Hurricane" played softly through the phone. I tapped a hand against my thigh. "You are like a hurricane; there's calm in your eye.

And I'm gettin' blown away to somewhere safer where the feeling stays. I want to love you but I'm getting blown away." I hung up the phone and rejoined the group.

A tiny saccharin voice laughed in the living room. Henry was standing beside his three-year-old godchild, whispering in her ear. The child was intentionally fatherless. I imagined he and the child's mother falling in love. Whenever he talked about them, he did so with nearly painful tenderness. The girl wore a pink dress and perched on a stool in the center of the room. She recited a poem with her eyes on a rug hanging on the wall behind the group. She looked down and Henry brushed her hair from the side of her face and whispered the ending to the poem. We clapped, and she flushed and hid behind Henry's legs. She ran to a girl who resembled her mother and yelped when she realized the girl was not her mother. Henry laughed so hard he wept as he scooped her up and delivered her to her mother.

CHAPTER EIGHT

# Unorthodox Worship

I began waking early on Sunday mornings to walk the city when group excursions weren't planned. I passed kiosks with wool bundled workers behind stands of potatoes, fruit, or pockets of hot bread filled with spinach or apples. I hiked down Prospekt Gagarina feeling light and happy as my black corduroys sliced the cold air. I passed the Dmitrovkaya Tower and a military museum. World War II had affected nearly every Russian family with the loss of a relative. Though my family never talked about the war, it had also affected them with poverty and death. My father loved pork and beans slathered with mustard, a "poor man's meal from Pop-pop's childhood," Nana would laugh.

Minin and Pozharsky Square was at the center of the city with buildings in elaborate nineteenth-century French Baroque. Traffic was closed from the square. Art shows slated Bolshaya Pokrovskaya (the main pedestrian walkway through the square) that led to Gorky Park, named for the famous writer Maxim Gorky who was born in the city. Until 1991, Nizhny Novgorod (then named Gorky) had been closed to foreigners for the security of Soviet military research. I brushed snow from the top of an iron gate before the statue of Gorky.

On Sunday explorations of the city, I went to Orthodox parishes, increasingly drawn to their somber beauty. I stood by a ring of candles and prayed with the priest's rich chanting and censing of the church. An experience of unexplainable holiness drew me to the Orthodox Church—so unlike the many churches I had experienced growing up Protestant. I slipped behind people with wool coats and covered heads, listening for how one responded to the priest's chanting. Some were silent, and some softly prayed the Liturgy. I smelled bread baking and felt the cold from a woman's coat. A young girl bowed to touch the hem of the priest's vestment as he continued down the church, spreading clouds of incense from a bronze ball the size of an egg.

One Sunday morning as the cold bore through my jeans, I entered the Stroganov Church of the Nativity. It was dark wood. A woman stood behind a cardboard box of rubles and another box of candles, and I felt her eyes on me. I had never had to buy a candle in church when we used them during Christmas Eve services. People made the sign of the cross and bowed as heavy sounds from the priest stirred the thick atmosphere. I felt weightless. An elderly woman breathed, "Lord have mercy." A red scarf covered a young woman's head. The priest emerged from the sanctuary doors. Frescos covered the doors at the front of the sanctuary. A spirit of warmth and light stirred inside as I fed from a circle of prayer candles. A woman rocked on her knees with a baby in a burlap sling on her back.

In Russia, the experience of "church" seemed completely foreign. Though I had prayed many times before in church, it had been in quiet times when the praise and worship band had paused for prayer, or after church with a prayer team. I hadn't experienced continuous communal prayer as it was in the Orthodox Liturgy. A person could barely hear the priest in the distance; instead, it seemed the people had come to pray through the service. I didn't think there was a sermon, but it was hard to tell with the Russian and the chanting and my eyes were closed in prayer.

Great peace filled my heart. "Lord, what an amazing place You've brought me to. Please fill me with Your Holy Spirit. Help me let go of all that is around me, to give myself to You. I am Yours." There was a tug on my arm, and I opened my eyes to the woman who had been selling candles. Her face twisted in disapproval with the tap of her covered head and the pinch of her skirt. My head was uncovered and I was in pants. I numbly pushed open the heavy door and afternoon light mingled with the otherworldliness in the church.

Unorthodox Worship 57

A beggar with milky-blue eyes sat in the snow a few steps from the church, his gnarled hand gripping a walking stick. I dropped rubles into his cup with the decision that I wasn't going to worship in an Orthodox church on subsequent Sundays, that I could pray in my dorm room and catch up on schoolwork. But peers would stop by to chat, so I left for Sunday walks to McDonald's. When I walked past Minin Square, continuing down Pedestrian Street and through the doors of another Orthodox church, when I slipped a new scarf from my book bag over my head, I thought I'd stop in one more time. Just to see. It was what I couldn't see that pulled me back in.

For six weeks each American student stayed with a Russian peer and their family. I lived with Natasha and her father in their apartment down the street from the university. Books and postcards from other American students were stashed in small boxes. Homemade curtains reminded me of Natasha's late mother, passed away with cancer. Plants were under the window. A bright sunrise streamed through the old room. It was almost spring.

I stayed in Natasha's room, a narrow space with pale walls. A bookshelf matched the dark wood floor. A full-length mirror on the back of her bedroom door surprised me with my own drawn face. Outside the window it was dark at six. It was comfortable to be in a home. Viktor Zsoy's mellow seventies music (bought for Dima upon request) piped through the recorder. Natasha's father shuffled past my room to the kitchen. Glass clinked glass, and I recalled the vodka next to pickled cabbage, canned vegetable spread, and an uncovered tray of sardines. I dreamed of mixed greens with avocado, tomatoes, slivered almonds, croutons, and grilled chicken drizzled in balsamic vinaigrette. I hadn't seen lettuce in Russia. I felt empty and began to pray. Natasha's father knocked on my door.

"Yes? — I mean — da?"

"Lea, soup? Ty khochesh?"

I opened my door and thanked him. He walked to his room, and I wondered if he would marry again. He played a sad record, and I went into the kitchen. A whole chicken and vegetables bubbled in an enormous pot. The chicken's feet were banded and bobbing at the foamy top. I ladled some broth and vegetables and returned to my room.

I first learned that Easter was "Pascha" while in Russia and that a mound of cheesecake sprinkled with raisins was called the same. It was Holy Saturday night, and Natasha and I rode the metro to Strelka Street. We were meeting Henry and others from the group at the St. Alexander Nevsky Cathedral for Pascha, which would begin at midnight and continue through the night. Before the church service began, the crowd stretched into the street where a man played the accordion and a woman sang in a throaty voice. A box to their side filled with coins and notes. Many people gathered around the church under a full moon. Natasha and I stood together as Holy Saturday dissolved into the dawning of Pascha. I held a smooth beeswax candle. "When do we light these?" I asked.

"Soon!" Natasha said. She leaned to my ear and told about the miracle of Holy Fire occurring on Calvary over the garden of Arimathaea. She said a fire appeared by itself every Holy Saturday when the Patriarch of Jerusalem entered the shrine. The Holy Fire was said to be mild, even safe to touch, and the people believed it was a material manifestation of the Divine's presence. "And when the fire doesn't spontaneously ignite," she paused, "it indicates the end of the world."

I wondered about Natasha's faith growing up in the Soviet Union. Surely her mother's death must have awakened fear and alerted her to the reality of mortality. Why hadn't her father come with us tonight? She didn't talk about faith in God or a relationship with Jesus, and I hadn't seen any icons or prayer books in her apartment that might have indicated she was Orthodox. Russians didn't seem to express faith in the same vocal ways as many did in Western Christianity. God began to seem far beyond description as I experienced Christianity in Russia. Scripture said to seek the Lord your God with all your heart, mind and soul. He would reveal Himself. Ultimately, faith was not without reason but beyond it and increased according to God's will as one cooperated in it. The experience of faith was as mysterious (and as real) as a candle flame.

The church doors opened and people tipped their candles to each other's; a soft glow spread through the church and down the steps into the street. It was well after midnight when people began feeding into the large church chanting Christ is risen! "Christos voskrese! Voistinu voskrese!" A priest shined in white vestments, hands raised above his head.

"Christ is risen!"

"Indeed, He is risen!" the people exclaimed.

It suddenly struck me: I knew nothing of the nature of God.

## CHAPTER NINE

# Meeting the Parents

It was my last day at Natasha's. As dawn broke behind the pink curtains, I slid my legs over a cool space on the sheets. Birds chirped for the first time in months. I tried to be at ease, but my body felt sluggish and unwilling. It was another day of transition, and I felt absolutely nothing.

Natasha and I knew we would likely never see one another again, and I did not anticipate an overly emotional farewell. She had been through host-student separation before. I was eager to leave, to be one step closer to home. Over breakfast of boiled eggs and thick kasha, she told me she did not think she would host another student. She said, "I fall in love with sister, and then she goes."

We went to the train station where the American students would leave for St. Petersburg. "I miss you," Natasha said before I boarded the train. Thoughts of meeting Dima's parents filled my mind. Hugging her, I inhaled sweet perfume. I gave her a Rock-n-Roll Hall of Fame snow globe, and she gave me a cassette of Russian pop songs. Her chin dimpled, and I turned and threaded through my peers.

After our overnight train ride, we were all relieved to arrive in St. Petersburg. I was still gathering my things when a man in a neon green windbreaker and cap stepped into the aisle carrying a bouquet of flowers. Dima's father walked nearer and our eyes met. His lips twitched with a controlled smile and he trembled in our embrace. He smelled of mint soap. As the group pressed to the exit, Viktor stepped back and motioned for me to go ahead of him. In eggshell quiet, we joined Tatyana and Grandma waiting beside the train. Tatyana hugged me tightly against her full chest, her thick hair tickled my nose. Grandma pressed against me from behind, and Viktor embraced our huddle.

"Welcome to St. Petersburg, Leeea," Viktor said in English. "We love you."

St. Petersburg was famous for Faberge eggs. Alexander III had the first Faberge egg made for his wife. The outside was white with enameled gold and inside was a golden yolk. Like the popular Russian dolls with miniatures inside, the egg was layered. The tsarina found inside the yolk a golden hen, inside the hen a tiny crown, and inside the crown a ruby. My experience of Russia similarly included many layers. The Orthodox Church, Dima and his family, and the culture of both were increasingly dynamic, and my interest continued to grow. In the process of being introduced to Russia, it seemed to me that God was revealing Himself more than ever before. There developed a strong urge to go deeper into this family and Christ. I stood beside Dima's parents and Grandma and felt connected to Russia as I hadn't before. Viktor asked Henry if he may take me to the hotel, clenching the handle of my suitcase under his large belly. Henry insisted I remain with the group.

My American peers seemed weary as we walked from the train and followed Henry to the Baltiyskaya Metro, which would take us to the Sovetskaya Hotel. Dima's father and I walked a few steps behind to be only a few more in front of Tatyana and Grandma, continuing at a pace of their own. I fell back with Dima's mother and Grandma and laced my arms in theirs. Tatyana looked different from what I had imagined. She was the same light color as Dima and seemed serious, her melodic voice proud and womanly. She wasn't tall but stood erect with an air of patience. She and Grandma had a similar scent that contrasted with my floral body spray. I strolled between them in nervous energy.

For the first time on the trip, the group had individual rooms in the Sovetskaya Hotel. The family opened my hotel windows and cool air fed into the small room. Tatyana placed the flowers Viktor had given me in a paper cup on the nightstand, and Grandma pointed to her watch. She told me I had twenty minutes before they would return to take me to their home. Viktor hugged me goodbye and Grandma meekly smiled and followed Tatyana to the hotel lobby. Silk scarves, a skirt, socks, underwear, and a pair of jeans scattered on the bed. I tore off my black pants and wrapped a long floral skirt over dark tights, smoothing the brown flowers wrinkled from having been stashed in my suitcase. I tied a matching scarf around my neck and pushed my hair into an amber clip. I found the crumbling remains of Secret Powder Fresh and smeared some under my arms, grateful Russians were used to more natural scent.

The family returned and I wasn't ready. My face felt greasy, and I hoped to wash it when Grandma's rapping persisted at my door. I grabbed a stick of gum and face powder. As I opened the hotel room door, Viktor chuckled and shook his head, his body motions telling me there was no need to get all dolled up. He offered some of his dark drink, kvas, as we made our way to the metro and into Kolpino. The drink was bitter and warm. Viktor's arm circled my shoulders as we made the last leg of our trip by bus into their city. "Okay?" he continued asking, which seemed a way for him to reassure Tatayana and Grandma that he was in control and I was taken care of. I smiled and nodded. Viktor unlocked the heavy door to their apartment and stepped aside. Dima's mother motioned for me to wear the red slippers in the corner. I sat on the floor to untie my boots.

"Nyet! Nyet!" Grandma shook her head, lower lip quivering. "Cold ground make infertile," Viktor explained in broken English. I stood, peering into Dima's room. It appeared unchanged with hockey trophies and ribbons. There was a tall bottle of water on the nightstand.

"Kioshka, Tmoshka?" The cats scampered to Tatyana in the kitchen as she leaned forward with a slice of chicken. She smiled and roamed her small hand across their orange coats.

"Lea! Tonya! Come living room," Viktor called. A table in the center of the room was set with red roses and pale china. Grandma sat at the table rubbing her ankle.

"Moma, juice?" Tatyana lifted the crystal decanter. Viktor patted the old sofa and I sat down beside him. A warming breeze from their small balcony sucked and billowed curtains. Viktor opened a children's book written in English.

"Viktor, study?" I asked. He nodded and smiled. He seemed proud but able to laugh at himself as he stumbled over simple English.

"On bus. Home sometimes." His words came slowly and he concentrated at length with each sound. I squirmed in our silence as he stared up at the ceiling with furrowed eyebrows. "Very difficult, very difficult," he said. They worked long shifts, sometimes through the night, and there didn't seem time to study English. He stepped over my crossed ankles to a cabinet for photographs. He scooted a pile of black and white photographs against my thigh. In one, Tatyana wore a miniskirt with a long braid over her shoulder. She stood next to a boat anchor at the Admiralty, a dockyard on the Neva River built by Peter-the-Great. It had been intended as extra defense against invasions after he first founded St. Petersburg, his "Venice of the North." Tatyana's youth fit there: dark eyes, soft face, and curvaceous.

"Here, Lea, me brother." Two men in naval uniform stood before a black gate, similarly dark haired, square faced, and lean. Viktor's arm was around his brother's shoulders. Behind them was a park decorated with marble statues and fountains around the Summer Palace. There was a smaller yellow palace in the back that had been built by Peter-the-Great for summer parties. The park was over three hundred years old, and it seemed astonishingly well preserved.

Viktor passed me a colored photograph of himself and Tatyana at the entrance to Dima's old sports complex. Tatyana's arms were crossed behind her back, and Viktor leaned against her. The cats gingerly sniffed my feet and darted under the table. "Take picture. Take picture for Dima," Viktor said, pointing to the cats. Tatyana had prepared fried pork chops, mushroom soup, and mashed potatoes. The table was spread with bowls of bananas cut in thirds, cucumbers and tomatoes mixed with dill and sour cream, and dark bread. Dima's mother nodded her head, and Viktor left the photographs and immediately took his seat at the table. I sat between Grandma and Viktor, Tatyana sitting at the head of the table and serving the meal in courses as we ate in silence.

"Spasibo, Tatyana. Ochen vkusniy." The food was delicious, but my stomach began to gurgle. I gingerly rose. Tatyana and Grandma looked up from their plates. I had not learned the word for diarrhea, and it was not the time for pantomiming. I studied the H-O-C-K-E-Y printed toilet paper from Mr. Holmes' visit years earlier.

Back at the table, Viktor rubbed his stomach, "Lea, okay? Sick?" I took the large black pills he held in his palm with a meek smile.

"Priviet!" Igor, Dima's cousin, announced, entering the apartment and walking past the bathroom. Igor was thirteen with silky blond hair he smoothed obsessively with a pink comb from his back pocket. His blue eyes and striking confidence spoke of unripe trouble. He approached the table and shook my hand.

"Is your homework done, Igor?" Grandma asked. He looked down, mumbling, "Grandma, I'll go back to your apartment and finish it later." I asked Igor if he'd like to see some photographs of the States. He followed me into Dima's room, flipping the album to Melanie and me jumping off the lighthouse at Mentor Beach Park. He pointed to my hair, flying up like a straight brown parachute above my body. Melanie's feet were just above the glassy water. Igor giggled, face buried in the album. I snapped a picture. "Ooh! Klasna!" he said, pointing to the camera.

Tatyana came into Dima's room laughing, "Leeea, Lea!" I followed her to the living room where the cats stretched thick orange bodies over the vase of roses. "Peeector! Peeeector." Her attempt at English and radiating joy warmed me.

Viktor called from the hall. He was poised under a small punching bag, fists in the air. "Tell Dima," he nodded. Tatyana refused to let Igor and me take a walk after dinner. Instead, Tatyana and Viktor decided the three of us would stroll through Kolpino after walking Grandma and Igor back to Grandma's apartment. The wind rippled the Izhora River. Viktor draped an arm around Tatyana and posed for a picture where they had first met twenty-three years earlier. We ambled over an iron bridge to the city's sports complex. Viktor pointed to a showcase outside the cement complex where there was a photograph of Dima in Findlay's orange hockey jersey beside a photograph of the 1990 Russian hockey team. I pointed to a boy next to Dima and asked if this was his best friend Sasha. They nodded. Families lived in apartments for lifetimes, and they continued to see Dima's friends. Sasha had become an alcoholic. Another childhood friend was divorced and also drinking heavily. Another, who had hoped to play professional hockey, was in the army.

On the way back to their home, we stopped at Tatyana's best friend's apartment. Olga stooped over small pots of herbs. She practically jumped up and down as we approached. "Friend Olga," Viktor said as we entered the apartment. Olga embraced me with fragile arms, slightly shaking; it was striking how different she felt from full and steady Tatyana. Viktor left for home, and Olga and Tatyana moved to the kitchen and prepared tea, voices just above a whisper. I stood alone in the room, green curtains stirred with a light breeze.

For a week, I rested in the overprotection of Dima's family. I took a shower one evening when the parents called from the kitchen. They stood behind three dishes of vanilla ice cream. We ate in peaceful quiet. I felt closer to Dima than I had in months. Later that evening, I uncapped the enormous bottle of water Tatyana had set on the nightstand. It was carbonated, preferred by many Russians, but I had never tried it. I tiptoed to the kitchen for boiled water and opened the fridge to leftover potatoes, a pork chop, a lemon wedge, and a basket of eggs. Tatyana appeared. "Leea, no like bubbles?"

"Oh, that's okay. I just want a sip of normal water." She didn't budge. "Tatyana, normalna, ya horosho," I tried to tell her everything was fine, but she went to the closet for boots and a jacket, pulled these over her nightgown, and left the apartment for the grocery around the corner. It was nearly midnight by the time I slipped into bed. The sheets were crisp and cool, and a flash of hand washing them came to mind. I had hand washed my jeans twice while in Russia, and it had required such a workout of scrubbing, wringing, and rinsing that I'd opted to throw them away rather than try washing again. Just then my thigh fell against peculiar wetness. The top comforter had a darker pink spot above my leg. The sharp odor confirmed it was cat urine. I sighed, paced the floor and peered around the corner into the living room.

"Ah, Viktor?" Covers rustled.

"Lea? Shto?" He followed me. "For shame, for shame!" he mumbled with a red face. Returning with a bucket of sudsy water, he peered up at me, rag in hand, and chuckled.

Though St. Petersburg was said to have only thirty days of sunshine a year, this week spent with the family there were four, and three in a row. When I returned for visits with the parents, Dima's mother heaped my plate with fish and potatoes, she poured steaming tea into a blue and white china cup that had become mine, just as the red slippers by the door. We shared strawberry wafers before bed and morning dishes of cucumber and dill salad.

Their apartment confined us in alternating awkward and easy moments. We didn't pray before meals. We didn't ask hard questions. We didn't speak fear, sadness, regret. We were simply there, together. Yet, I continued to need to say many things: I love your home. Thank you for letting your son leave. How could you? Did you know it would be years before you'd see him again? When will you come to America and see him, meet my family and the Holmeses? Do you want to live in the States? Do you want Dima to move back home? Instead, silence. Until a translator came for dinner.

A frail woman sat across from me. Sweat beaded Viktor's forehead. Tatyana didn't smile when the cats jumped on the counter for the raw chicken. "What are your plans with Dima?" the translator asked with a somber look.

"I love him. I — I think we'll get married."

"What do your parents think about this?"

"They love Dima. They were worried when I said I was coming to Russia. They definitely don't want me to live here. But they know how important Dima is to me. They see that we get along well—that we balance one another. They aren't opposed to my marrying him, I don't think." My parents and I hadn't yet had this talk. "My parents see he is a good man. They trust my decisions." I wanted to explain my faith. In desperation, I said, "I am a Christian — I will love him. I will love you. I can't explain —"

Viktor's voice was harsh and matched his steely face, jowls reddening as he cupped his chin and looked far off. "Why would a group of American students want to come to Russia? What is in it for them?" the translator asked.

"We want to learn about the country and the people." Dima's father seemed skeptical and cold for the first time, and I was afraid, realizing how different our worlds were and how difficult it was to communicate my spiritual and emotional motivations. At the same time, I was filled with hope, joy, and love — passionately brimming with faith in God and family.

On occasions, Grandma escorted me from the hotel back home and Tatyana greeted us with a full smile. After we had our slippers on, she motioned us into the living room where we watched a video of Dima playing hockey in high school. Grandma and Tatyana beamed, adding Russian words to the English cheers. Grandma and I sat shoulder to shoulder on the couch, and his mother disappeared into the kitchen to prepare bliny for dinner.

Viktor walked through the door, "Ellow?!" Grandma turned her head with a smile and made the sound she always did, "Aooo." I hugged Viktor, his body odor strong as he embraced me. He hung his coat and reached into his pocket. Tatyana appeared from the kitchen, and he threw a piece of bubble gum at her chest, laughing as it hit her bosom and fell to the ground. She looked at him, unsmiling, which seemed to make him laugh harder. He leaned his head over his round body to her pouting lips and kissed her. She accepted the gum he picked up from the floor.

Grandma and Viktor watched TV and Tatyana cooked. Being there was like being at home when I was little — afternoon fading through the drapes, sweet pancakes for dinner, Russian style. My mother had made pancakes and sausage with fruit cocktail some nights. Before Tatyana left for her night shift at the factory, she brought me her robe. "Lea, cold?" I smiled and slid my small body where her full figure had been and sat down for dinner with Viktor. We ate in quiet and nostalgia evaporated. Time ticked slowly. Viktor waded through a stack of pancakes four inches high, finally leaning back in his chair and sweating.

"Music? I like Beatles," he told me moving into the living room for a tape player. We listened to "The Beatles Greatest Hits" and continued sitting at the table.

"Lea?"

"Da?"

"You, ah, um — doter. You are my daughter." I hugged him.

"I vant boys. Five boys play hockey," he said. The phone rang.

"Ellow, ah Dimka!" Viktor motioned for me to pick up the phone in the living room.

"Dima?" I curled on the recliner in his mother's flowered robe and stared at the rug hanging warmly on the wall. He asked how I was, what I'd been doing, and we both gushed how we missed each other. As we continued talking in sappy, young lover ways, he said that he had been praying for me. I believed we would someday make a very warm home together.

The next morning, I gathered my pajamas from Dima's bed and jammed them into the suitcase. Tatyana knocked on the door and came up to me with swollen eyes. She offered a small box. "Viktor," she paused, a hand covering her mouth, swiping her cheek. "Wedding ring to Dima," she managed. A thick rose-gold band was on top of gray tissue paper. Viktor wanted to begin a tradition of passing the wedding band through our family. What would it mean to become a multicultural family? I felt numb, overcome by a flood of emotions. In quiet moments on the metro, walking to and from the hotel room, and in late night silence, I nurtured hopes of being back with Dima and beginning the long journey that I believed we had share.

I also felt burdened by a weight I couldn't explain. It was not love for Dima, or marriage, or supporting his family in coming to America. All of these, even then, seemed things I was willing to do. I sensed there would be much beyond my control. If I chose to marry Dima, this lack of control would become a new way of life. I desired an opportunity to grow and change, but wondered about the very personal cost of marrying Dima. I wondered what marriage might mean in general, and to Dima specifically. At the end of a journey through Russia, it seemed that if Russia came to stay I might have energy only for some of it, will for some of it. Without God's help, there was no way to imagine sustaining life in love and peace. Love, when I couldn't understand another; peace, when life was seemingly out of control — lessons had yet to be as hard as they might become. Though I felt a hint of fear, there was more joy and excitement in being together with the boy I loved. I believed very simply that we would make a life together, and that it would be good, centered on the Lord, and enduring till the end.

I tucked the white box with the wedding ring into a corner of my suitcase under a wool sweater and hand-painted marble box. I wouldn't look at it again before handing it to Dima. Somehow, I even managed to forget about it with the anticipation of my mother's hug, lilacs blooming in Ohio's spring, a long walk under the moon with my sister. The wedding ring didn't belong in my life — yet.

It was late April when our group left St. Petersburg. We met at the bus station at five in the morning. Most of us had stayed up through the night talking, saying farewell, preparing to return to the worlds we had left over four months before. It seemed hard to believe how much had changed in such a short time. I still felt the adrenaline from our arrival in Russia, the thrill of a wildly new place, and the overpowering sense of hope and belief that coming to Russia was God's will. We had fifteen minutes left in St. Petersburg at the Pulkovo International Airport. I leaned my head against the bus window and heard a soft knock. I had expected Dima's parents to come, even though it was hours before dawn. I lunged over legs and into the aisle and stepped from the bus.

*Meeting the Parents*

"I love you," I said wrapping my arms around Dima's parents. My coat was unzipped to the early morning chill on their jackets. Tatyana breathed warmly against my neck. Viktor pinned an amber broach to my sweater. It looked like a leaf dipped in honey. "Thank you, Viktor." He nodded and sadly smiled.

"Leka, tell Dimka we love him," he said.

"I will. Ya budu, ya budu." As I left them to rejoin the group Viktor called, "We miss you, Leka!"

*Dima and his mother in Kolpino, Russia*

*Author (sitting) and her sister Melanie*

*Dima's (goalie on team's right) in Kolpino, Russia*

*The Holmeses' house*

*Dima in high school*

*Dima and the Author*

*Dima and the Author*

*Wedding rehearsal dinner. Author's parents (left) with Peter and Sharon Georges*

*Meeting Dima's family at the Saint Petersburg train station*

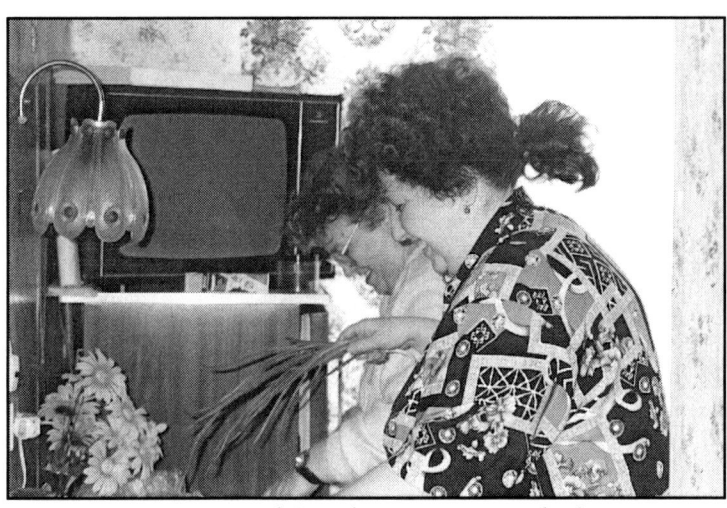

*Tatyana and Grandma preparing author's
first meal at their home in Russia*

*American group in Red Square, Moscow*

*Cook at the dormitory in Nizhny Novgorod*

*Natasha and her father in their apartment in Nizhny Novgorod*

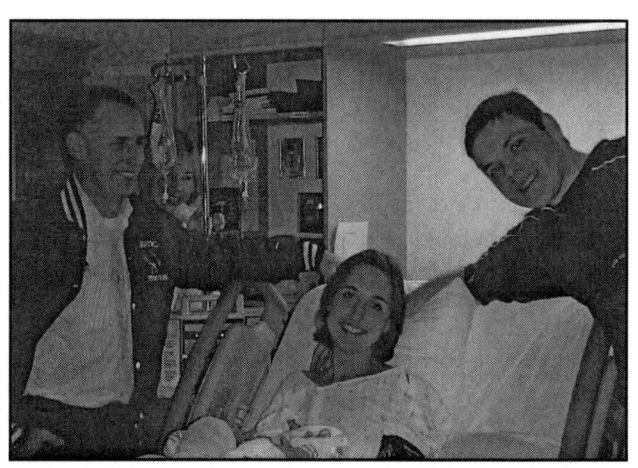

*Author's father, author and Dima after delivery of Viktor Jr.*

*Celebrating Dima's U.S. citizenship wth the Holmeses*

*Dima's father with Viktor Jr.*

*Author's in-laws, Viktor and Tatyana Povozhaev,
with grandson Viktor Jr.*

*Baptism (Author, Fr. Andrew holding Viktor Jr., and Dima)*

*Dima, the Author, Viktor Jr. and Dominik*

*Author with Viktor Jr.*

## CHAPTER TEN

# Marriage

Four months after stepping into Dima's embrace at Cleveland's International Airport, we vacationed with the Holmeses at their summerhouse in Upper Peninsula, Michigan. Dima slipped his arms around me from behind as we paused from a walk through the woods on the Fourth of July. Day filtered through a canopy of leaves, and the day was comfortably warm, scented by the conifers. In an accent strengthened with emotion, Dima asked me to marry him.

I could do without a bended knee proposal. With the Holmeses' Independence Day party that evening, there would be a roasted pig, champagne toasts, and fireworks. With Dima and me, things were simple. Calm. His kiss was tender. He led me from the woods to the edge of Lake Huron rhythmically lapping warm sand. I leaned against him. His chest was warm and his heart beat strong. He smelled naturally sweet, a hint of salt above his lips. We were easy together with the sound of the water, the feel of the sun.

His parents came to the States for the first time to celebrate our wedding. His father sat on Dima's bed in a red and black checked robe with his chin in his hands and breathed deeply. I backed out of the Holmeses' and left for my parents' house. We were to be married in a matter of days.

"I don't know," my voice broke. His parents' visit, a stretch of six weeks, was almost up. The mantra repeated: savor now. Think of Dima and his family instead of yourself. It's been eight years since he saw them. The internal argument came easily: they hang sheets over windows, slurp soup, refrigerate peanut butter. His mother inhales jellybeans with wine.

With the Holmeses and my family, Dima and I seemed to be understood as a couple. We were asked, even more, I was asked, how we felt, what we thought, how things might be done. It seemed I had more control of the bringing together of our lives and families. With Dima's parents, there was a void of communication. It was greatest with me, but a lack of explanation and mutual understanding seemed also to wedge between him and them. Most obviously, it was the language barrier, but on a deeper, more troubling level it seemed his parents didn't really perceive my place as Dima's soon-to-be wife. It could almost seem they had mentally and emotionally maintained him at an earlier point in time, before me. I expected to have time and attention alone with him. When his parents were with us, I expected to be considered and naturally integral to Dima. I couldn't fathom the differences between us that felt heavy and divisive. Unlike the rest of the family who had shared the past five years as Dima and I fell in love, cookouts, Saturdays at the beach, holiday parties at the Holmeses, had not included Dima's parents in a physical way. Phone calls hadn't communicated our family dynamics. While meeting them in Russia had introduced us to each other, it all seemed quite different in America with Dima and without familiarity of their homeland.

Our ways of living were vastly different. They seemed slow and dramatic. I must have seemed fast and selfish. However, Dima and I were absorbed in great hope of our approaching marriage, which lessened the cultural divide acutely experienced between us and his parents. Still, his father's jokes, meant for Dima alone, seemed to hang hollow in the air at times. His mother's resistance to the rest of the family and, together with Viktor's, constant cleaving to Dima pushed against my own desire to be near to him.

"Mrs. Holmes, I love Dima — and his parents. But. This is so hard…" Susan squeezed a clothespin over wet shorts, her face concentrated.

"How long did you stay at Sea World?"

"We were there from eleven till eight. Honestly, I was really trying to be patient. I mean, we stared at the seals for two hours! It wasn't so bad until around six. That's when I started hinting we needed to leave. But Dima would not speak up! He's driving me crazy."

"Maybe he didn't see a reason to. You weren't there all that long." She rummaged through the utility room for a clothes basket.

"Well, by eight we had been, and I said so. Tatyana was mad at me. She wouldn't look at me or talk. I could tell, she was thinking I was a selfish American."

"How do you know that? Maybe she was just tired?"

"No. When we got into the van, she was actually pouting. And when we stopped for gas and I was alone with them, I couldn't handle it. As soon as Dima got back, I made him translate. I told them I was sorry, but it was getting late."

"It wasn't that late."

"I know. But his mother actually said that I have childhood playing in my butt, whatever that means." A subtle smile rested over Susan's face.

"Do you want a glass of wine?" she asked.

Dima and I were married at Mrs. Holmes' Lutheran church July 1, 2000. The church exploded with lilacs and Easter lilies, which Aunt Caroline set around the sanctuary in her untucked T-shirt and jeans. I arrived and walked through the kitchen; the bridesmaids were arranging flowers, dressed even more casually, as was I, in a pink tank top and cutoffs. I was giddy with excitement. My sister and our childhood friend stood side by side wrapping flower stems in moist tissue. Our friend had had her first child weeks before. She squeezed me and made a growling noise in my ear as my sister laughed. Peace filled me as I slipped away from everyone to get dressed.

I had no doubts. It was an experience of simple bliss, senses heightened by the quickened pulse of celebration, by the chance to express the sure love Dima and I shared. Our family was together and supported our union, and it all seemed so easy, nearly unreal. I thought of my dad with a strange stir of emotion. Though I longed to be Dima's wife, it was a step that distanced me from Dad and Mom in ways I didn't yet understand—ways I didn't necessarily fear but anticipated as necessary change. Change was slippery, exciting earlier on but hard to sustain with faith and peace. I was leaving a family that loved me in understandable ways for a family whose ways of loving were no less, but different. Dima's ways were unexplainably calming, and I looked forward to finally calling him my husband and beginning the next stage of life that had come.

In the lobby, Dima's mother and mine wore matching pale dresses and appeared nervous as they stood together in silence. Both had teary eyes when I walked towards them in my white gown. Our fathers wore tuxedos. Viktor's face was flushed, and his body rigid. My father's face was masked; he didn't like being the center of attention and nerves silenced him.

Susan and Caroline arranged bells, ribbons, and flowers, waiting till the last minute to apply glossy lipstick and simple dresses. Mr. Holmes slipped into the sanctuary a step slower. He had been the host of our rehearsal dinner in the Holmeses' backyard, serving foreign liquors through the humid summer night. My Aunt Vicki wore tiger-rimmed glasses on a chain around her neck, Bible in hand, marked to the passages she'd read in the ceremony.

After the processional, "Trumpet Voluntary" by Henry Purcell, Peter Georges sang a contemporary praise and worship song, "Shout to the Lord." His voice was strong, traditional. Though I'd never heard the song sung in such a way, it felt right. Six bridesmaids and groomsmen in matching sea-mist and lavender began down the aisle. My heart pounded in silence, arm strewn through my father's. I barely breathed as we moved to the front of the sanctuary where Dima stood with a fresh haircut. There was a rustle as family and friends stood. My father and I turned to each other, and he lifted my veil and kissed my cheek. The tremors in my heart surprised me, and I choked back a full sob. Though biting back tears, some escaped and mingled with a dripping nose. My sister and cousin giggled. With everything in me, I aimed to be still and control the intensity of the moment. Control was shaky but present. Dima and I followed the pastor up a step to light unity candles. I stumbled, and those in the sanctuary inhaled. Catching myself with a giggle, I turned and mumbled, "I'm okay."

Before the candle, we held hands. We prayed, "Lord, please bless our marriage. Be the center of our lives and guide us together in all things. Help us to be pleasing in Your sight." At the end of the marriage, Purcell's "Trumpet Tune" played through the recessional.

After the ceremony, Peter Georges shook Dima's hand. "Congratulations!"

Sharon hugged me. "Beautiful wedding," she said.

Still in the church, Dima and I held hands before emerging to the people waiting outside for us to run through their toss of rose petals. "I love you," I said, and he smiled, called me Mrs. Povozhaev. "Finally!" We kissed and ran.

Our reception was at Mentor Harbor Yacht Club. I feared Aunt Caroline was ill with her mouth and teeth the color of crushed blueberries. She wished us a happy life together with a genuine smile, Merlot on her breath. Family and friends formed a circle for the bride and groom dances. I leaned my chin against my father's shoulder, closed my eyes and breathed his sporty aftershave and skin, imagined his blank expression, bottom lip half sucked in, slight smirk concealing any sign of emotion. I was the spitting image of my dad and could make him mad past words. I felt oneness with him that broke and filled my heart at once. Days before the wedding, he had told me that my premature birth and the fear of losing me reminded him throughout my life how much he wanted me to live. He said it was a good test that never let him take my life for granted.

I opened my eyes to Dima dancing with his mother. His eyes met mine as his mother nestled her face in his chest. Her full shoulders bobbed in the expensive gown she had begged Susan to return. The sun was setting bright orange above the lake and seeped through the windows. I whispered, "I love you, Dad," and moved to meet Dima.

After our wedding, honeymoon in Maui, and college graduation, I imagined Dima and I would somehow have money. Even my parents had more than we'd ever had growing up. They took two-day vacations to cabins in the woods to ski and began updating their house. Things quickly settled into a more realistic perspective. We spent our first summer together in my apartment near Malone, living on yams and spaghetti. Soon the semester began, and we endured weeks of separation as Dima finished his coursework at Findlay while I completed mine at Malone. We graduated and saved our money, working odd jobs and living in an apartment in Findlay. The apartment was above a bakery and smelled like fresh bread, but many things were less appealing. The apartment complex was near a mental health facility and housed some of its patients. The apartments were one room flats with tall windows, no screens, some of the windows barred over. We set flower pots on the sills overlooking the city.

I wanted a house and a full-blast shower head. Our apartment was on the third floor and barely had water pressure. Other things bothered Dima. One neighbor rarely closed her door, and we heard her softly singing. When Dima looked across the hall, she was naked. He hung blankets over the two windows that — oddly enough — faced the hallway and added locks to our flimsy apartment door. After a year of my teaching English at a private school and Dima working a construction job, we finally had just under ten thousand dollars for a down payment on a home.

We house hunted with two things in mind: location nearer the Cleveland area and no more than $120,000.00. It was late winter, typically dreary. Our bad moods boiled under the surface, comments snapped. I told him I didn't care where we lived so long as we finally moved. When we saw an "Open House" sign in the front yard of a gray bungalow in Stow, Ohio, we stopped.

"This is actually a party for cosmetics," an amply shaped girl smiled. I hadn't applied makeup and felt as bleak as the day. "We are selling the house, though. My mother's not in right now, but I'll have her call you. If you'd like to, feel free to look around." Other than the pea-green carpet upstairs, it was a nice starter home and Dima thought it had potential.

Like much of life, we fell into the next pattern of our days. The home had been selling for fifteen thousand more than we were able to spend, but the woman agreed to settle with our offer and said she hoped we made it our home. The day we moved, I slipped through the passenger side door of the U-Haul, laughing with a sense of youthful recklessness. Dima told me to calm down, but he was also giggling. We stopped at Cracker Barrel for dinner, and I ordered milk for the first time in years. I felt strangely like a child, and yet more grown up then ever before. We were going home.

He maneuvered the truck over our driveway, the back end as close as possible to the side door where wild roses were in bloom under the kitchen window. We walked to the front door holding hands and Dima unlocked the door. "I haven't had the chance to do this," he mumbled, stepping behind me and telling me to jump a little.

"What are you doing?" I laughed as he cradled me in his arms and moved us both over the threshold. We paused in the empty house before turning on the foyer light. There was the faint smell of disinfectant and garlic. A sense of goodness seeped through me. We huddled together by the front door and prayed. We asked God to make our home a welcoming place. Though there was a mess to sort through, piles of our separate lives that had yet to blend, all that belonged to tomorrow. That night, we made love on a blowup mattress in our new living room.

One Sunday, not long after we had moved in, Dima drove through a nearby town and we stopped at an Evangelical church next to Mc-Donald's. "There's a breakfast," I whispered. Pancakes and bacon drifted through the morning. A sign welcoming visitors was taped to the glass door. Dima suggested McDonald's instead, but I insisted we try to find a church to attend. We meandered back into Stow, and he pulled into a parking lot around the corner from where we lived. The church gleamed white against manicured flower beds. We sat next to a bright girl in the sanctuary. "Welcome to New Grace," the girl said. She was the pastor's daughter, my age, and a teacher. Our friendship was easy, though it seemed Dima felt as uncomfortable as he had at

Malone. He introduced himself as Dimitri and remained as closed to our new community as I was open.

My parents had decided church was "for the birds" and seemed to be taking a spiritual hiatus as Dima and I settled into our own Evangelical community. Melanie and Joe and Dima and I sat at Mom's new dining room table. Dad's fried fish steamed in the center. My father looked to me and said, "You guys are where we were years ago searching for the perfect church." I disagreed, wished he'd really listen to what I felt. In the glass quiet, I wondered if we were praying before the meal. "I guess I'll say a prayer," my father said. "Lord, we thank You for this food and ask You bless it to our bodies. We pray for our loved ones. Amen." I choked down the fish and pushed Dima out the door for home. On the drive to Stow, thoughts of Dad's dry prayers made my throat thick.

Aunt Vicki and I grew closer. We began writing letters and calling one another. When in town, she visited our church. We shared morning coffee and Bible devotions on overnight stays. She fit in with New Grace. It was more than her dark lipstick and exuberance, which matched my new friends', more than her raised hands, closed eyes, and whispered "I love You, Jesus." The Evangelical Christian culture there matched what she had been a part of since saying the "Sinner's Prayer" in her early twenties. I was excited to share such a close bond with my aunt, especially because tension seemed to be growing between my father and me concerning religion.

My aunt and I pondered why my father refused to visit New Grace. My father would say, "These Evangelical services are like going to concerts." Yet such churches seemed alive to me. Animated people with bright faith. Such communities moved people from stagnant relationships with God to personal love of Jesus. My father had recently been attending an Episcopal church. The stained glass was pretty, but I couldn't understand the deeper appeal. I tried to accept that tradition made the liturgical services meaningful for the trickle of congregants, mostly aged, that attended my father's new church, but the services felt flat. I didn't experience the rhythm of the church.

Unspoken tensions changed relationships in our family. My mother became a chain link between my aunt and me and my father. I knew Dad was annoyed and I was increasingly sensitive to his disapproval. It wasn't easy to cut up veggies in my parents' kitchen for the dinner salad without a glass of wine.

I complained about my father's reticence on the phone with a friend from New Grace one evening. "I think your Dad is a Christian —" What did she mean? I knew my father was saved, even though it was true he seemed distanced from what I'd known Christianity to be. I hadn't been able to talk to him about faith, and especially church, since weekends home from college. He seemed to be closed in ways that I couldn't understand. Nonetheless, my father and I had prayed for Jesus to come into my heart when I was three years old. Beyond that, on an intuitive level I knew he believed. If abandoning the need to seek the Lord was possible, I doubted the belief had ever been grounded in the soul. My father had to be searching still because I believed his soul knew the Lord. He was just angry. Yet the fog of cynicism and disgust that darkened him was physically painful to me. He was not open to talks about church because he thought he had tried them all, and they had all failed him.

After Dima and I had been at New Grace nearly three years, my parents came to the annual church picnic. It was a humid summer afternoon, and breeze through the pavilion circulated smells of chicken, potato casseroles, and brownies. The pastor's wife said to my mother, "Don't worry about a thing. We'll take care of your daughter. We're so happy Dimitri and Lea are at the church." My father looked as bored as "Dimitri." My mother smiled, her face glowing from a day on the boat with my father. She wore a salmon blouse, her arms warm with sun. Dad stared at the paths leading into the woods with the inside of his bottom lip clamped in his teeth.

We finished eating and my father stood to leave. I whispered that we could go swimming or hiking through the woods, if he liked. He said he had some work to do in the yard. My mother said, "Donny, I'll help you with that. Let's take a walk before we go." We walked in silence batting mosquitoes from sticky legs. I looked up at Dima who stared ahead.

"Do you like the people at our church?" I asked my father.

"Lea, they seem fine. Do you?" My father usually said what he really meant, no matter how obnoxious. The walk was brief before my parents left.

While New Grace had become a community of friends for us, it was at the same time a culture of protected distance. Problems that didn't go away in a timely fashion seemed kept from view so they wouldn't hinder others from feeling "comfortable" at New Grace. There was a lack of diversity, as though unity were built superficially instead of in the universal life of Christ. I wanted holiness and life in the Spirit. I prayed with a friend there for Spirit and Truth. Was there a way towards Jesus Christ that transcended life situations, that was beyond problems; a holiness that had depth and that, when lived, assured greater hope in salvation than my own thoughts and feelings offered?

There was a welcoming team at the church that greeted people on Sunday mornings. Dima and I stood post once a month, but he soon found another job (working Pastor's Powerpoint presentation) on most of our assigned days. He was unwilling to smile on cue. I wanted real community, enduring and honest. I wanted faith that could heal and save, as it had in ancient times. We prayed and expected miracles, but there was something disconcerting about unanswered prayers. It seemed there wasn't a sound way to endure and suffer in the culture we were a part of, but I believed such steadfast faith was a part of the life the ancient Christians had experienced.

We took our burdens to Jesus, one on one. The church taught people to behave as individuals, to maintain accountability to Christ alone. Our way to Jesus was through our understanding of the Bible and His will. It started to seem impossible. How could there be sustained responsibility to what a person perceived God expected? Wouldn't there be times when we got it wrong? What guided faith that was beyond my thoughts and feelings? I wasn't comfortable basing faith on what changed. I feared God and wanted nothing more — and nothing less — than salvation.

As a child, I'd sung a church song: "Trust and obey, for there's no other way, to be happy in Jesus, is to trust and obey." However, it began to seem that such trust and obedience needed a strong, spiritually-based reality. Fractious churches with divergent rules and friendly cultures that seemed more concerned about earthly things than the kingdom of God would not foster lasting trust and obedience to God. Furthermore, spiritual joy was deeper than earthly happiness, which was often dependent on life's circumstances.

Before children and Dima's parents came, wedding pictures and pale cylinder candles were on my childhood dressers in the guest room of our bungalow. There was a tall iron lamp, left as trash by the past homeowner, in a corner by the bed. In the thick of summer, with skin like melting wax, we'd trade our bedroom upstairs for the saggy bed of the guest room. We lay in comfortable silence, summer pushing through old windows open and unlocked through the night.

Dima and I absorbed quiet moments in the crimson bedroom and dreamed of filling the baby's nook, a pinched space with bleached wood and Noah's Ark. Old fashioned Christmas lights lined the bar in the basement. A tattered plaid quilt draped the futon beneath pillows that smelled faintly of Dima's scalp and cinnamon. Knobby antiques were gifts from Aunt Caroline's house sales.

Before the family came, he watered house plants and I made coffee and oatmeal on Saturday mornings. There was often a phone call to Russia, Marc's 500-minute calling card turning in his square fingers, long legs crossed, chords of Russian playing through the kitchen. I loved the sharp sounds spoken in his soft voice. I was transported back to my travels in Russia, reminded of the longing I'd had, and had still.

It was a wet, late autumn morning when my Aunt Vicki came with us to New Grace. "We want to pray with the prayer team for fertility," I told her. We were in the throes of treatment, countless internal exams and possible solutions that didn't seem to be working. Hormonal imbalance made anxiety and sadness slick and physical.

The doctor told me to be still. There would be no running or aerobics, no way to alter brain chemistry. Whirlwind fear filled my mind.

Dima and my aunt and I joined an elderly Frenchman named Michael at the front of the church for prayer. He took a small bottle of oil from his pocket and mumbled that he wanted to anoint us with it. He unscrewed the plastic top and crossed our foreheads with shaking fingers. I hadn't seen the prayer team anoint people with oil before, but I believed in Michael's faith. He placed his hands on our shoulders and Aunt Vicki held our hands. Michael began to pray. His accent was thick, words came slowly. A prickling sensation moved up my back. My aunt squeezed my hand and whispered pleas to Jesus as Michael spoke. Dima was pillar still and silent. The heat from his hand burned in mine. Afterward, we were silent. My aunt prayed, "I believe they will have a son, and he will be an arrow in the heart of the enemy. Sweet Jesus, thank you. We believe."

"That was powerful," Michael said. I was trembling with emotion and faith. When my aunt told me the words hadn't come from her and she felt the message was from the Lord, I believed her.

The chances were slim, and I didn't feel that different, just sharp pains in the mornings. My abdomen had been swollen with the hormone injections, so bloating couldn't be counted on as a sign. The doctor had been realistic, "It will be difficult, maybe a seven or eight percent chance," he had said. Laughter was hollow for weeks.

"I believe it will happen, Lea. I don't know when but I have faith." I thought it was easier for Dima who hadn't physically undergone seven months of testing. I thought of unfinished graduate school and the barren bank account, but then the notion of our child filled my heart. I prayed, "Above all else, Dear God, I beg your mercy. If it's your will, give us a child." In my heart, I realized that I might never conceive, but rare peace replaced fear.

Midway through two weeks of waiting, I was dusting the basement and on the phone with my sister when she said, "I'm just really tired. I, ah, don't feel that great." I was nauseated and cold.

"What? Are you pregnant or something?"

"Well, actually, I am." Silence.

"Oh — Melanie, that's wonderful! I — I," a sob lodged the words.

"I'm so sorry. I feel awful. Me and Mom didn't know how to tell you."

"Oh, please don't. Please don't ever keep anything from me. I'm happy for you, really. A baby —" Anger and jealousy alternated with hope and love, and emotions moved quickly. When I hoped to also be pregnant, a glimmer of natural joy met my sister's. In anger and self-pity, life was dark.

Dima and I returned to the advanced reproduction and gynecology office at the end of April. There would be months of waiting if we proceeded with treatments that would cost thousands of dollars. "We could take out a loan —"

"Just relax. We don't even know if you're pregnant or not yet." I thought Dima's optimism shallow. The doctor's office was luxurious, which made me think of all the money he received from patients like us. He had two pictures on the wall of strawberry blond children with their mother. His chair was enormous and loomed high above his balding head. "I want to do surgery before we move on. Your uterus is shaped slightly abnormally." He drew a picture of an upside down triangle with a nominal dip at the top. He ran through the other test results that had been normal and said we'd go ahead and do a pregnancy test today and then an exam.

"Dimitri, you're welcome to join us in the exam room." He stood and said he was going to work. He had only taken an hour of paid time off. I kissed him, not at all minding that he was leaving. There was no need to draw all this out. I felt strangely calm and accepting as I filled a plastic cup with urine and changed into a flimsy robe. I sat on the exam table and stared at a caricature of a woman with a toothpick waist and hips like two C shapes on either side. In pointy gloved hands she held a chained tiger.

The nurse entered with a smile. "Lea, the consultation may have been for naught. You are pregnant." Everything went blank. I laughed and trembled, staring at the nurse in disbelief. Warm tears wet my face. The nurse handed me a plastic tube with two blue dots at the top. "It's a clear positive. You can keep that." She slipped out of the room. The doctor entered and said he was happy for me, but his smile held carefully in the corners of his mouth.

I hardly believed as I drove home with hands numb on the steering wheel. I slipped from the car and into the kitchen. In the warm afternoon, I eased to the ground with a sensation of seeping past myself. "Lord have mercy," I breathed. On the side step by the rose bushes I ate a bagel with butter and strawberry jam. The day was light and breezy against my arms. The rose bushes had buds, and an infusion of color would spread across the side of our home. A squirrel scampered for an acorn that had found its way to a pothole in our driveway. The cordless phone was beside me. "How should I tell him, Lord?" Nothing dulled the deep peace and unrelenting joy. I had never lived a miracle such as this, had never desired something seemingly so far from my grasp.

I picked up the phone. "Dima, yes, I'm positive — I am pregnant. Of course the doctor confirmed it. Why don't you believe?"

With our first son, I knew God had given us a child to share with the world, and particularly with family. Joy was the strongest emotion, but a sense of responsibility began to surface. Our wills had matched, but I had to be careful not to limit God's work to merely satisfying my desires. His plan was beyond mine. Yet, I couldn't help but believe He had taken me seriously. He had heard my cry and answered the desire of my heart. I wanted nothing more than to abide in Him.

Dima and I began the endless path to becoming parents. "Lea, did you see this?" He entered the computer room where I was typing with a yellow and red paperback that had been on our shelf from someone years before. "It's on the differences between Russian and American childrearing."

"I haven't had time. Besides, I'm exhausted. I don't even want to think about all that." There was graduate school, three baby showers, teaching; there were bathrooms to clean, furniture to dust, meatloaf to make at ten in the morning when I was starving. All piled like a blurring mound of responsibility that I might have chucked for the sake of long hours of rest. The more to do, the more I felt I had to push myself. There was no time for patience with Dima.

"I'm telling you, it's really good. I think we should both read it before Baby comes," he said.

"Look. After you read it, then I'll read it." I figured it would be behind our bed collecting dust alongside his other books: a Russian war memoir, Michael Savage's *Liberalism is a Mental Disorder*, and Tom Clancy's *The Bear and the Dragon*. He cocked his head to the side, straight-faced, and charged me. His fingers wedged under my arms as he tickled me. "Stop! Sssstop," I laughed.

"You have little woman syndrome, you know that? I've said it before, and I'll say it again — Balls said the Queen! If I had them, I'd be the King!" I slipped from the office chair onto the old carpet.

"Come on. Please, stop or I'll —"

"What, what can you do?" Laughing, he pinned me down.

"You're hurting the baby."

With the swelling of my womb, hope and possibility seemed endless, enough to swallow any differences, any obstacles.

Nana had come from Florida to visit, and we drove an hour north to Melanie's brick ranch for a pool party and cookout. The family circled the pool, while Nana reminisced.

"I remember when your mother told me that Melanie was stealing your blankie. I had said, 'surely, Diane, she's too little for such antagonistic behavior,' unable to believe it! And, sure enough, she was just seven months old and you, Lea, just nineteen months, but she'd scoot over, wiggle herself on top your blankey, and laugh. Why, I'd never seen anything like it!" I smiled, moved my painted toenails through the cool water. Melanie and I had always been close, and being pregnant only two weeks apart seemed nothing short of a miracle.

"Are you going to come into the water?" Melanie asked.

"You're a total fish. I'm not in the mood to swim." I felt cold, hungry, tired. Even pregnant, she seemed so carefree. She wore her plaid two-piece, small belly beginning to show.

"Do I look fat?"

"Well, fatter. I mean, we are pregnant," I said. When we were little, I used to tell her to suck her stomach in, but she'd arch her back and let it go, not paying attention.

"Have you been taking it easy," my mother asked me, chewing the inside of her cheek as she did when she concentrated or worried. She leaned forward towards the dog, "Nono!" She grabbed the beagle's collar and pulled him from her burger. He whined and snapped at her hand.

"Ponch! Bad dog!" Melanie lifted herself out of the pool. "Are you okay, Mom?" Our mother just smiled, biting back any comment that might upset Melanie and Joe. She was always the peacemaker.

"You have to get rid of that monster before the babies come," I said. Joe's brown eyes met mine from across the pool.

"You know, Reverend Leroy Zimkey told me you would become pregnant," Nana said, shifting her round body clad in golf shorts. "He said that once you were still and relaxed it would happen." My father sipped his bottled Budweiser and looked at me with a weak smile. His dark hair was peppered with white, but he still had a youthful body, strong and healthy like his father's. He looked on the brink of boredom and irritation. I was sure he was itching to walk the block home and paint a plaster fish.

Summer fed into fall and finally winter. Dima and I watched the baby's elbow under my taut flesh on lazy evenings on the futon in the basement. Boxes of baby necessities collected by the bar: diaper genie, bouncy seat, highchair, most of which needed to be assembled. "But when are you going to do it? We don't have that much longer, honey. I really want everything set so there's less stress when Viktor is actually here."

"I'll do it soon, okay? This weekend." I wondered if our son would have a still and patient nature, veering toward lazy at times, or live on the edge of his seat, jumping to the next thing. Would he be tall and quiet like his father — or small and dark like me? Would he learn Russian? Would he be convinced that colds came from cool air against one's neck, that garlic was the cure-all, that only boiled water was safe to drink even in America? How would Russia separate me from my son? And how would our son change the dynamics of our family?

I had heard the stories. "My father left home when he was fourteen, after eighth grade," Dima would say. "He was on his own, like me. It's in our blood, woman." I silently wondered about the mixing of our lives that began to seem more different than ever before.

## CHAPTER ELEVEN

# Changing Perspective

"In the life of a man a miracle does not happen just by chance. It is given depending on spiritual necessity and on the influence it will have on that man's inner world."[1]

Two days before Christmas, 2004, I delivered Viktor. My father leaned over the hospital bed peering at him. "Look, Dad, he's wrapping his fingers around my index finger. He's strong." A mix of emotions began to break from the confusion inside.

"So, you want to do this again?" my father joked. I told him not for a while, glancing at Dima heaped on the couch, chin cupped in his hands. "I bet Dima's up for it!" Dad laughed.

"Nana says congratulations, and she can't wait to see her great-grandchildren," Melanie said, shuffling from the phone to my bedside, cradling her newborn. She leaned down and wrapped an arm around my neck, hugging her baby between us.

"I love you, Lea, you too, Viktor." Suddenly, my sister seemed older to me. Our parents and the Holmeses milled about the hospital room, vying for their first glimpse of Viktor.

"The snowflakes are beautiful—big and light. Make sure you write that in your journal. Viktor should know what a beautiful day today is," Melanie said. Everything seemed surreal—from Melanie holding a baby of her own, to holding Viktor, to Christmas Eve the next day. Viktor's life was a true miracle, which I would never forget.

---

[1] Vera Bouteneff, trans., *Father Arseny: A Cloud of Witnesses*, fourth expanded edition (Crestwood: St. Vladimir's Seminary Press, 2003), 226.

Friendships at church began to fade. Pastor and his family faced personal problems, and people left the church. Christian unity in the Evangelical tradition seemed more shallow than ever before. At New Grace, Holy Communion was random and occasional. It was a time to reflect on Jesus and one's personal sins. However, if we were one in and through Christ, what did this mean for Christian community and the Church? Our unity was not maintained and defined by the sacrament of Holy Communion at New Grace, but it seemed it should be.

After service one Sunday, Pastor walked over to us. "How are you, Dimitri?" He shook Dima's hand and hugged me.

"Not too bad," Dima said.

"Any news from your parents?"

"Yeah. I talked to them the other day."

"How are they?"

He said they were okay as I interrupted, "His father's in the hospital. They're doing all kinds of testing. They think he might have had a stroke." Pastor's smile faded. "I mean, he's only fifty, but men's life expectancy is fifty-five in Russia." He shook his head.

"Are your parents saved?"

"I don't know," Dima said. "We didn't talk about religion growing up—"

"I think his grandmother is," I offered. Pastor waited. Dima said nothing more. I cringed inside.

"Aren't you glad you're in America? Without Christianity, there is the greatest suffering. Russia is a prime example. I might have a Bible in Russian for your parents."

I thanked Pastor and squeezed Dima's arm. I went to the restroom. It was pink and berry and reminded me of Pastor's home. It was scrupulously clean and organized. In my experience, if you weren't a friendly, bright-faced American, it was difficult to fit into the Evangelical culture, and I could see why Dima might not have felt a part of New Grace. However, Christ came to save all people, from the East to the West. Cultures of Christian faith had many looks, but it was Christ Himself that transcended the world and unified Christians. I wanted to be where there was the perspective that the world was within Christ, not where vain effort was made for Christ to be in my world.

The ancients experienced supernatural encounters with the divine. People hadn't as many rational explanations, and perhaps the mystical was more acceptable. To hear God, one had to listen. After Christ's crucifixion, Saul was on his way to Damascus to continue persecuting Christians when a blinding vision and God's own voice asked him why he was doing such things. In astonishment, he remained blind and fasted for three days. In a dream, Ananias of Damascus was told to go to Saul (later Paul), heal him, and share the news of Christ. Though hesitant, as Saul was known for fiercely persecuting Christians, Ananias obeyed. Paul's zealous nature turned to serving God with the Christians, and he set up the first churches. Early Christians endured physical discomforts, from fasting to martyrdom, and by their lives (and in some cases deaths) miraculously showed Christ's power.

Paul set up ancient churches, similar to the Jewish temples in structure. Animal sacrifices were no longer necessary as Christ had become the sacrificial lamb and completed the old covenant. Christ fulfilled the law and offered the Christian perspective sustained by the Church. People confessed sins before the congregation, partook of Holy Communion, and were baptized in the Holy Spirit. In addition to the Church's sacraments, fasting, giving alms, confessing sins, and praying were Christ's statutes, established in the Church from the times of the first apostles. It seemed there would have been an atmosphere of reverence and obedience. Much had changed from the ancient Church to New Grace. Modern Evangelical Christian culture began to seem more worldly than spiritual.

After five years of marriage, Dima's paperwork finally processed through Cleveland's immigration service, and he was going downtown for an interview to become an American citizen. Our seven-month-old Viktor slept, and the morning rang with quiet. My breath rippled the coffee, steam on chin and lips. Dima stood in a pinstriped suit studying naturalization papers as the cat rubbed against his slacks.

"Loosen up a little, there's no reason you'll be denied citizenship," I said and slipped my arms around him from behind, breathing in Dove soap.

"Nothing is for sure."

"I love you. It's going to be okay. One step at a time, babe, one step at a time." He turned, and I reached around his neck and whispered, "Thinking about your parents?" He nodded against my shoulder.

I waited in an upstairs room in one of Cleveland's high-rises as Dima became a U.S. citizen, bouncing baby Viktor on my leg. A woman from Greece was beside me, and her silver bracelets jangled as she fidgeted with her immigration papers. A father and sons from Moscow smelled of sweet cologne and wore slick pants. There were many families and some individuals. Most appeared tense as they spoke in their native languages with family. I was proud that people from around the world wanted to live in America and imagined how difficult it would be to leave one's homeland.

Dima was issued citizenship, and we rejoiced together. I told him I didn't care what conditions we found ourselves in, I'd never let my children leave the country without me. He said I didn't understand because I was an American. I couldn't imagine needs so great that my family would disperse but trusted God had a plan in allowing Dima to come and stay in America. I was grateful his parents hadn't forbade it.

Despite the relief and joy of Dima having become an American citizen, his parents' summer visit became a whisper, they're coming, they're coming, they're coming, pulsing under the louder parts of the day. They would come for one month, August to September. They would fly into New York where Dima would pick them up in Aunt Caroline's minivan. They insisted on the sixteen-hour drive to and from New York. "It will give us time to catch up," he told me. I didn't argue but had mixed feelings about not being a part of the initial excitement. Sixteen hours of driving with a toddler was out of the question. I would stay home, all agreed.

I should have anticipated this brief respite as a time to be still and prepare within myself. I continued running instead, feeling that the pace of our life was too fast to suddenly pause. Saturday morning coffee and oatmeal, making love and limitless plans was traded with the endless responsibilities of work, school, and baby — life seemed a juggling act. I began to feel like a machine. Our relationship that had always included tender touches began to seem mechanical.

Dima was at work and I was organizing our life, paying bills, making lists. I called Susan Holmes to confirm our trip to their place in the Upper Peninsula with Dima's parents the next month. We tried to plan ahead but more often than not our day to day responsibilities muddled together. Everything seemed haphazard. Determining where to attend church had become like a sandbox, granules of thoughts brushed here and there. We visited a couple Orthodox parishes and it seemed time was necessary to understand. Time I felt we didn't have.

One Saturday before they came, Dima sipped instant coffee at the table as I prepared oatmeal, like the good old days, only neither of us felt good at all. After his father's stroke, the doctors feared he would have a heart attack. He didn't play racquetball twice a week, walk after dinner, or limit his diet. He was nothing like my father. "Is he going to be healthy enough to come? I mean, what if something happens while he's here?" I said.

"I don't know — don't worry about it. It'll work out."

"Well, will he have some sort of insurance?" The phone rang. "Figures. Whatever." I dumped oatmeal into the boiling water as Dima paced the kitchen with the cordless phone. I listened to their conversation by translating his tone and watching his hands, recalling some words and phrases I'd learned. He was talking about New Grace. His father had called last week to tell Dima he was getting baptized. His father had asked, for the first time, if we were "believers." Dima had said we were. He called my name as I stirred raisins into the oatmeal.

"What denomination is New Grace?"

"It's an Assemblies of God church — why?" I turned to him grinning above my old robe. He waved his hand for me to be quiet and turned to the kitchen window. His mother asked where we were going to church because she had spoken with a priest in Russia who had asked if the church was Protestant. The Orthodox priest wouldn't pray for us if it was. I was defensive. "Was your mother even baptized with your father at the monastery last week?"

"I don't know. Dad went alone." His eyes fixed on his empty coffee cup.

"Want more?"

"Not really." He looked distant.

"Aren't you glad to talk to your parents about the Lord?"

"Yeah — but, it's weird. We never talked about this stuff growing up." I couldn't imagine and wondered how his parents would react to church in America. A faint prayer began for faith that would draw us together.

Before his family came, we visited an Orthodox parish close to our home on a Thursday evening. A curling drive took us a quarter of a mile from the road to a silver domed church. It was not a church a person would accidentally find. It seemed tucked away from the world, though it was big with a loud bell. We slipped into an office in the basement of the church. A man taller than Dima with a large forehead greeted us from behind his desk. He wore a tee-shirt and warm-up pants. We introduced ourselves and squirming Viktor and settled in chairs before his desk. He looked to Dima and asked about his past in Russia and current situation.

"Protestants are so confused, many don't even believe in the Trinity," the priest said. "In grade school, my son's Protestant friend told him Christmas was just a story and that the Christ child was make believe." By the end of the night, he handed us a rule of prayer, an Orthodox calendar, and an envelope for our yearly pledge that would need to be given before the baptism. I tried to understand, to roll with his assumption that we would be baptized. I could at least entertain the idea of becoming Orthodox. Otherwise, the entire evening seemed a waste.

We walked back to the car with Viktor fussing on my hip. I scuttled my sandaled foot against the dusty parking lot. "I just don't know about all of this. Why should we have to pay in order to have Viktor baptized?" I said.

"They have to keep the church running. I think it makes sense." Dima's voice trailed off, and I thought he too wondered. We had planned on tithing but were on a fifty-dollars-a-week budget for groceries. Moreover, I believed in the Christ child along with my Protestant friends and family.

We returned for Divine Liturgy on Sunday. The choir loft was above us, and the music was powerful. We rustled diaper bag, purse, bottle, and infant carrier into a pew. I took comfort in the familiarity of older members' crossing and chanting as Dima and I passed Viktor back and forth, cooing, bouncing, rubbing, anything to keep him from before-nap-time fussing. To no avail. Concentration was impossible, and I took Viktor to an empty room with toys and books. A young girl joined us and I asked her if there was a Sunday school for the children. She said Sunday school was before Liturgy. I calculated the length of Sunday mornings: hour-long Sunday school, hour-and-a-half Liturgy, and then coffee hour, an optional time of socializing. It seemed a little over the top to me.

Dima stood quietly, concentrated, even stoic. "What, you can't hold my hand?" I whispered.

"Shhhh. This isn't time to cuddle," he snapped. In the priest's brief sermon, he encouraged the people to live the Faith through the upcoming fast. I wondered what people would be fasting for, and what fasting actually meant. Did people go without food? For how long and how often?

"What did the priest mean about fasting?" I asked a woman behind me after service.

"Oh, Father's new here. I don't know what he's talking about." I tried not to judge, tried not to surmise this early on that people were only going through the ritualistic motions. We followed parishioners downstairs for coffee. A young woman offered her name and asked ours, offering a handshake and cautious smile.

I babbled on with nervous energy, "I'm a Christian. I've been saved since I was three." The young woman smiled, sipped her coffee. I took her lack of conversation about salvation, mine in particular, to mean that she didn't believe me. An attractive deacon a few years older than us weaved confidently through the people.

"Welcome to our parish," he shook my hand, a sheet of paper over a magazine. "May I get your names and address?"

"We're just visiting. We go to a church in Stow right now," I looked at Dima who appeared ready to offer all of our information for their records. "My husband's family is coming from Russia for a visit this summer—"

"From Russia?" His eyes bulged. The paper that had been over the magazine fell to his side. I nodded matter of fact, less and less thrilled with the idea of it all.

"That's the Georgeses," I gawked at the cover of the magazine with African children.

"You know these Ugandan missionaries?" the deacon asked.

"They've been friends of my family's for years," I said.

"So," he looked from Dima, to me, to our son in the carrier with a full smile. "You must be Orthodox?" he said to Dima.

Outside in the sunshine, Viktor in my arms, we drifted through a field on the side of the parish. "This is it. This is where I want to go to church," Dima said. I nodded and looked into the bright day. I wasn't sure I agreed with him but a calm kept me quiet. Questions and doubts clouded my mind, but my heart seemed unnaturally patient. I was drawn to Orthodoxy. There was something different and real here. I wanted to be sure it wasn't the novelty of the Faith but the truth. I still had yet to come to terms with one holy catholic and apostolic Church. This was a large hurdle to pass having spent twenty-six years Protestant.

I called Sharon Georges days before his parents came. "We're returning to Uganda at the end of the month, so any time before that we would love to have you over," she said. We had a million things to do: plant the tomatoes, cut the grass, buy shrimp and wine—and an immediate understanding of Orthodoxy would fit between one and four on Sunday afternoon. We agreed to visit the St. Nicholas Orthodox parish they attended in Mentor that next weekend.

At St. Nicholas in Mentor, I felt more comfortable than I had in other parishes with friendly, American faces and other children there. Afterwards, we dropped Viktor at my parents' and walked down the street to the Georges'. Their home was familiar and warm. Peter and an African from the Ugandan seminary where Sharon taught sat on the deck under an umbrella. "Are you studying for the priesthood?" I asked. He said he was and in a heavy accent explained how the many Ugandan dialects limited the ministry.

"How are your parents?" Peter asked Dima.

"Excited to come." I sensed Dima wasn't in a talkative mood as his body stayed relaxed with a quick answer. I felt uneasy. I had known the Georgeses as a child but not as an adult. I began to care what they thought of Dima and me and our families in ways I hadn't thought to as a child.

"May I use your restroom?" I said, as much to force Dima to converse as to calm myself down.

"Come on in," Sharon said through the screen door in the kitchen.

"Can I help you with anything?" I asked.

She was washing her hands in the sink, nails a dark mauve. "Oh no. During fasting seasons we eat simply. We were just going to have some pasta a little later, if that's all right?"

"Sounds good." I was starving. We had skipped breakfast and it was going on two. I returned to the porch where she offered Kool-Aid and set crackers and cheese under the umbrella.

"We've been praying for your parents for the past nineteen years, ever since we left the Evangelical church we'd gone to with your folks," Sharon began. "We never thought you would figure into this."

"I didn't expect to either," I laughed, feeling shaky.

"Your mother seems hesitant, but your father is interested in Orthodoxy," Peter said.

"Really? I don't know. Dad's been frustrated with religion for a while now. We had always talked about the Lord, but for the past few years we haven't. I mean, for a while now my Dad's prayers have seemed so un-heartfelt. It doesn't seem like he is praying."

Peter told me to stop and a pained expression creased his forehead. He shook his head before looking away. I hadn't meant to disrespect my parents and hadn't realized how deep their care for my parents was. I apologized with tears in my eyes, and conversation turned as Peter and the African talked about Uganda. There were many difficulties in educating the Ugandans such as the different dialects, limited number of dorms, and many medical and family needs. The people suffered with HIV, and many students had relatives and parents dying or passed on.

"Life is so easy here," Peter said and sighed.

I looked at Dima, who remained mute, and begged him with my eyes to speak. Instead, I filled in the silence. "I like myself better when I'm pushed. I'm less self-absorbed. Like when I was in Russia. Someday, I would like to do mission work." Sharon nodded with understanding.

"It was a challenge to leave everything here. Peter was making good money in business, and to let go of that opportunity took some time," Sharon said.

"When we first left as missionaries, we had plans and goals that didn't wind up as planned. We had to realize that it would be God's will working through us, not simply accomplishing our plans. That's why we came back at first, unsure if we'd carry on as missionaries." Sharon's eyes glowed. She looked the same as she always had — powdery skin and soft hair, rounded features and intense smile. "It was perfect timing because when we came back to the States, we learned Peter was ill. If we hadn't come home, he wouldn't have had the care he needed."

The same house and yard as my parents', the familiarity of shared years, despite the lapses of time within those years, and the hope in mutual faith made time with them precious. I could have stayed for hours longer, but Dima sat on the edge of his seat and spoke of having things to do. Of all the times in our life that he had sat back, I couldn't believe that he was pulling us away from the Georgeses. If it hadn't been that I was dying for a salad and my mother's brown sugar Pop-Tarts, I would have weaseled us into at least another hour.

My parents were sipping instant coffee on the patio when we walked back for Viktor and lunch. "What did you think of their church," my father asked, pulling the screen door open and sitting at the kitchen table. He didn't even pester me about rummaging through his refrigerator, or "stealing" his favorite Pop-Tarts.

"It was long—but, Dad, it wasn't bad. I mean, it was weird with all the chest crossing. I couldn't follow the Liturgy, didn't know what to say or anything. But, I really like the way the sanctuary feels." St. Nicholas in Mentor was welcoming, seemingly open to our family and eager to invite the children and me, as much as Dima, into fellowship. The people sang the hymns and seemed engaged in the Liturgy. I wanted to understand how they lived this ancient tradition. The priest was welcoming, though not pretentiously so. His smile reached the corners of almond eyes, and his handshake was not loose or so tight it seemed he was trying to exert power. When he spoke with us, I sensed his love was sincere and earnest.

"The people are really nice there," my mother said, thinking of the Georges' girls' weddings years before.

"If it wasn't so long, so involved, I think I'd go to St. Nicholas," my father said to my surprise.

I remained curious about Orthodoxy for the sake of Dima's family and with a bizarre sense that my father approved of it. I was confused by the differences between the Orthodox and Protestant traditions, as it had always seemed to me that a Christian wasn't defined by a church. I defended Protestantism, to Dima, to myself. But a small piece of me was already accepting a sense of Orthodox Christianity. Still, I was parsing through spirituality, trying to measure the pieces and parts and make sense of a mystery.

The very first time I called Father Andrew from the Georges' church, I asked him if he'd be willing to baptize our son. "Yes. I will baptize your son. But the baptismal ceremony welcomes a child into the Church, and it becomes the task of the parents, along with the

Church, to raise the child steeped in the tradition of Orthodoxy," he began. I was not planning on that. "So unless you plan on raising him in the Church —"

I wanted to hang up and forget the whole thing. I would just have to explain our situation to the family. I had never believed baptism saved one. I had always thought salvation was in accepting Jesus into my heart. I didn't believe in working my way to heaven.

I asked Father, "How does the Church interpret salvation?"

"The Church teaches that there is not a single moment when we become saved. Our lives are the lifelong process of becoming saved, and in death we will be saved. Salvation's a process. And baptism is a promise to live that process. The promise is important but not a ticket into heaven." He said compared to the East, the West had a harder time embracing the mystery of faith because the culture had grown dependent on logic. We had learned to live more dependent on man and less so on God. Moving past understanding and into the realm of belief, which was inherently beyond comprehension (though certainly not without understanding), was made difficult, if not impossible, because of a sense of self-sufficiency.

Though I was put off with the exclusivity of one Church, I couldn't settle. I continued calling Fr. Andrew and he talked with me, introducing Orthodoxy in small pieces. "The Protestant tradition contains some Orthodox principles, though not all, and only through Orthodoxy is the fullness of Christianity experienced." He spoke gently but his points were firm. His words were clear, and his confidence was reassuring. He didn't try to persuade me. It seemed he knew the depth of the human soul could not be convinced but rather led by an example of one's life in the Spirit. I trusted him. If I entered the Orthodox Church, it would be with a spiritual father who understood that my Protestant past was not void of Christian truth but who also seemed to be experiencing a fullness in Christ, which I longed for.

There was something different about Fr. Andrew and the Georgeses that encouraged me to continue seeking Orthodoxy. They seemed quietly aware of their imperfections and more patient with others'.

They seemed to have a quiet confidence. Everything about the difference seemed interior. I had known many wonderful, believing people who looked perfect. I wasn't interested in Christianity that was limited to culture, not mine, not Russia's. Christianity was more, and though I didn't understand how worship at St. Nicholas might reveal this, I thought it might.

After telling the pastor at New Grace we were leaving, I sank into our mattress and curled into a ball facing away from Dima's warm body. I wanted to melt into a softer place. At times, becoming Orthodox in twenty-first-century America was countercultural and alienating. However, the majority of Christians, from the time of Christ to the present and throughout the world, were Orthodox. Inseparable from the Church, from the followers of Christ that were guardians and witnesses of Tradition that went back to the Apostles, the faith wasn't about culture, politics, or social standing. Becoming Christian was all about life in Christ. Still, there were times I feared judgments, prejudices and falsehoods in the name of Christ. What was the truth, and could I ever know it?

# III

## CONVERSION

"[C]hange is properly defined as conversion, a word that at its root connotes not a change of essence but of perspective, as turning round; turning back to or returning; turning one's attention to."[*]

"[W]hen He, the Spirit of truth, has come, He will guide you into all truth; for He will not speak on His own authority, but whatever He hears He will speak…"[**]

---

[*] Kathleen Norris, Dakota: A Spiritual Geography, (New York: Houghton Mifflin Company, 2001).

[**] The Orthodox Study Bible, New King James Version, First edition, (Nashville: Thomas Nelson Publishers, 1997), Jn. 16:3.

## CHAPTER TWELVE

# Parents' Summer Visit

It was a breezy August night. Our bedroom window was open to the sounds of crickets and owls. Dima was in the hall rocking Viktor and telling a story about a Russian fairy tale character, Baba Yaga. "She is a witch and eats little children who stray through the forest and into her hut built on chicken legs. She can be a mean grandmother when her little ones don't fall asleep. She doesn't cook well, even worse than Momma's leftover casseroles." I chuckled. He crawled into bed beside me.

"Thanks for putting him down, honey." He looked at me with an expression asking what his good behavior might have earned him. I traced his forehead, cheek, jaw with my finger.

"Don't do that. It tickles."

"You're such a baby," I laughed and turned the light off. He wrapped his arms around me.

"So, Mrs. Povozhaev, is this my reward?"

As Dima drove the borrowed minivan to New York City to pick up the family, I couldn't sleep. Instead, my mind filled with the five of us sitting at the kitchen table clinking champagne flutes. The clock chimed 2:00 AM when the Povozhaev Express finally rumbled up the drive, the American flag flapping against the white post.

Dima's father Viktor stepped out of the van first, hugging me tightly but careful not to press my chest against him. His face was less full than it had been five years before. He stood straight, hands down by his sides, and looked at me with a playfully serious expression and modeling his fifty-three-pound weight loss. I told him he looked good. His chin had lost a few layers, but there was still a hearty belly to fill.

I wiggled myself into the stuffy vehicle past Grandma's cane and bags and she kissed my cheek. She was shaking slightly. Tatyana squeezed my bare arm from the backseat, "Leea, Leea, Previet!" Dima's mother and I strained toward each other. Grandma gripped Viktor's arm and slowly stepped down from the van. Gray slacks slid past her swollen ankles. Tatyana followed, warm night moving her thick hair and patterned clothes.

I ran to the back of the van to help unload, but Dima and his father took all of the bags and shooed me away. I led them through the polished kitchen and into their bedrooms. Grandma set her plastic bags down in what had been my office. She ferreted through her things for a yellow and red tea set. "Beautiful, Babushka. Very beautiful." I silently wondered about my gift to her, eying an Orthodox cross embroidered on a thick cloth above her bed.

Before they came, my mother had asked, "Where will they sleep, honey? Won't it be too crowded?"

"Mom, they are used to cramped spaces. They live in one bedroom apartments. It's totally different. They can't expect what Americans might." It seemed to slip my mind that I was, in fact, quite American. One kitchen and two bathrooms would not be enough.

From the fridge, stocked with four times our typical amount of food, Dima helped me pull shrimp cocktail with lemon and crackers and cheddar cheese arranged on a china dish. Heavy smells of body odor sifted through the essence of our small home, overpowering the lemony scent of Murphy's Oil Soap. Tatyana emerged in her tiger print bathrobe, and Dima's father whistled. Grandma shuffled into the kitchen, short gray hair brushed back in an owl like puff. Viktor opened the pantry and then a closet, seemingly interested in what lay beneath our lives in this quiet town. He sighed and sat down at the table, silver cross on his bare chest. Dima mumbled behind us at the sink.

"What's wrong?" I asked.

"Champagne's flat."

"Nichego." Grandma insisted on drinking it flat, but we filled our wine goblets with boxed Cabernet Sauvignon. I was still expecting a Russian-style celebration: robust toasting, eating, joking. Silence hung in the room like the heat, even though it had been fourteen years since Dima, Grandma, and his parents had all been together.

I left the loud silence to wake eight-month-old Viktor. Maybe I kept them from speaking Russian. Viktor's arms hung limply on my chest, his soft breath on my neck. "Hey, little guy. Are you ready to meet the family," I whispered. He stirred and opened wide eyes.

We entered the kitchen, and Dima's mother said, "Leea, nyet." She shook her head and frowned.

"Lea, why'd you do that? Put him back to bed. Why would you wake him?" Dima said.

"I just thought it was a special—"

"Noooo. Leea, Veektor tired. He sleeping," Dima's father explained, head cocked.

I buckled him into the highchair with shaking hands. Our baby laughed and reached out to his grandfather over the tray. I warmed a bottle as Grandma smiled, touched a warm palm to his tender cheek, "Aaaaoo."

"Vitka?" Tatyana called, scrunching her nose, puckering her lips.

I had begun stashing questions in a notebook for when Dima's parents arrived, but my questions were replaced with theirs. Where are the crackers with morning tea? What's the temperature of the freezer? Do you have a bucket and scrub brush for hand washing Grandma's stockings? With the buzz of Russian, natural smells, and busy kitchen, our home began its conversion.

The spaghetti boiled. "Shoot. Dima, your Dad can't eat carbs, can he?" I had forgotten about his Russianized Atkin's diet.

"It's fine. He just won't eat much of it," Dima said.

"I made a ton! Great." I stirred the chunky tomato sauce. "I think there's a lot of sugar in this—will it upset Grandma's diabetes?"

"Very delicious," Viktor said at the picnic table, his plate swimming in sauce and a few noodles. My notebook was by my plate. I looked up at Dima for translation, but he was busy with noodles. I interrupted his feasting.

"Right now?" he asked.

"When else, honey? So, how did you end up staying with the Holmeses longer than a year?"

After a clipped response from Tatyana, Dima said, "You have to ask me that question."

Try less personal, more political.

"What do you think of President Putin?" His father breathed deeply and looked off into the dusk.

"Human life is not worth a dime. People are killed for a cigarette. Many are afraid of the police, maybe even more than criminals, because the police have the power to take things. If a police officer likes a car, he can make up an accusation and take it. The elderly are killed for pension money, which isn't enough to live on. President Putin doesn't have the power to change any of this or help the people. Communists run the black market. The only way to have anything in Russia is through cheating."

His mother added, "The Hermitage is very beautiful! You must visit in the summer, the flowers and fountains are breathtaking." Her face glowed and her eyes were glassy, from the wine or emotion, it was hard to tell. Her lips were full like Dima's, and her face was relaxed the way his always was. "America is so young compared to Russia. The Orthodox Church has only been here two hundred years. The Church has been in Russia since the eleven hundreds." I asked if his family were believers, but he didn't want to get into that right then. It was difficult to converse at a pace set by Dima.

"What did your mother think about your being baptized in Susan's Lutheran church?" I asked. Susan had recently given me a cassette of his baptism. Protestantism taught that baptism was only a symbol of one's faith. My father had baptized me in the lake when I was a child. I hadn't grown up with baptism being central to life in

Christ, though I was beginning to wonder about the depth of meaning in holy baptism.

"She was opposed to me being baptized outside of the Church. But glad I would be baptized in some kind of church rather than not at all," he said and passed the cucumber salad to his father. It was late. Grandma sighed and took a long sip of tea, looking beyond our driveway into the night sky. Her face was as smooth and calm as water. Her housedress was unbuttoned under the rickety table.

Our first excursion through town forewarned me of the endless battle I faced to be patient. "Where are we going?" I asked. The Povozhaev Express had already made stops at Rite-Aid, CVS, K-Mart, Marc's, Famous Footwear, and Payless Shoes. Each place had seemed another exciting bargain for the family with possibilities such as finding Grandma the extra-wide shoes she "could never find in Russia." According to Tatyana, they didn't have the selection I took for granted and often avoided.

By the time we landed in the parking lot at Walgreen's, Dima's father insisted that Grandma rest in the van and I stay to watch her and Viktor. I resented the fact that I had been forced into a role that presumed full watch over Viktor (never mind Grandma). We waited in dense humidity. After a half hour, Viktor ambled to the van, concern creasing his forehead. "He hot, Leeea. Very, very hot," he said pointing to the baby.

"It's okay. I will give him his bottle. It's almost feeding time." Viktor shook his head with worry. I didn't know what he expected. Too much air from a fan or air conditioner and the family feared the baby would get sick.

"Where are we going?" I called from the backseat to the front of the van where Dima and his father sat.

"I have no idea. I'm totally confused," Dima said. After some discussion, we drove the short distance back home with the windows closed in the back of the van. Air rushed through the half opened front windows.

Back home, I snapped Viktor into the highchair, made a bottle, and rummaged through the pantry. What can I make them? Quick.

Easy. "Don't worry about food," Dima said. "I'm going to grill." I was starving and pulled a box of instant mashed potatoes from the shelf. I sat at the table stirring a mess of microwaved potatoes and spinach.

"What are you eating?" Dima asked. Viktor stared at me sipping hot tea, sweat rolling at his temples. Dima gathered the lighter and cooking spray. "My parents are going to think we eat like crap!"

"Look, I'm living — not putting on a show," I snapped as he slipped out the side door, letting it slam closed.

It was a new morning, but it felt like another hour to the day before. The family had stayed up late with Dima laughing and sharing stories. I had drifted off to bed before the rest of them, banking on the time alone I'd have the next morning.

"Get up! I can't handle all this without a little time alone. I mean it. Please, Dima. I'm going running. When Viktor wakes, you have to get up —" he pulled a pillow over his head. I yanked it from the side of his long jawbone. "Don't you think it's reasonable — I'm just asking for one hour to run and pay the bills. Alone. In peace. Pleeeease?"

"Whatever," he spat. I stomped from our room into another morning. I didn't want to fight. At the very beginning of the family's stay, the frenzy had been exhausting and strangely exhilarating, but it was quickly sizzling into fury. It began to feel like we were wasting away. In the first days, we had still laughed and found time to be together, if only in a calming embrace in the upstairs bathroom. Until Dad interrupted. He had needed Dima to teach him how to cut the grass.

"What does 'ATM Adjustment' mean?" I mumbled at the computer screen. Dima was in the kitchen making a bottle. "Negative ninety-three dollars?" I called my mother. She transferred one-hundred-fifty into our account.

"I'm glad I can help you guys out," she always said. Yet it made me mad. It was hard not to blame everything on Dima, but with a glance at his tired eyes, my heart broke.

"Is everything else okay? You and Dima getting along?" my mother asked.

"I do not want his parents living with us. I know that already."

"You've got to be patient, sweetie."

"Dima and I are all right. Don't worry about anything, Mom. Everything's fine, or it will be. I'm sure." My mother's quiet pronounced her overbearing care. She held her words inside, but I heard them in the silence: What will his parents do in America? Where will they live? How will you and Dima have time for each other? I wished she took fewer of my troubles upon herself. Did she believe that I could handle it, that my love for Dima and commitment to our family would endure? I needed her faith, not her worry. Yet, I always gave my troubles to her instead of holding them in.

Within days, the family had our eight month old rolling around the crumb laden floor, sipping tea from unwashed spoons, and sucking lemons from their tea. Dima's father stood beside our bed with a smile. "Dima, hey, baby? It's time to get up," I whispered, looking up at his father.

Tatyana and Grandma took to sipping Labatt Blue beer while chopping fish, chicken, and cabbage dishes for our dinners. It wasn't said until his mother had had a few beers: "What does Lea cook? You look thin, Dimka."

After a quiet dinner, red dish cloth in hand, I faced the kitchen bombed with grease and shavings of carrots and potatoes. "So much for Thanksgiving dinner, huh?" I had planned to give them a feast. Dima's eyes were glossed. Maybe it was the shot of Vodka, sneaked from the freezer; the physical closeness of his family; the tension between our life and theirs. He was theirs. He was mine. I stared into his gray eyes.

"Look at the kitchen. There's no way I can get in here and put together a turkey and stuffing and all that crap." Besides, I didn't know how to stuff a turkey, and it didn't seem important to learn anymore. I leaned against the dark countertop before launching into scrubbing the refrigerator handle, stovetop, sink; before putting the clean dishes away from the dishwasher, scraping the crust from the newly dirtied and reloading. I shot a dirty look at Dima as he yawned.

"Russians know hospitality better than Americans," he said to me on more than one occasion as the family lived with us.

"What's that supposed to mean?" He didn't explain, but he did not have to. By the side door, a minimum of twelve shoes and slippers cluttered a quarter of the kitchen. Fish stained the counters, even after scrubbing at six in the morning before the family awoke to catch my quirky cleanliness. Used tea cups and tea bags, chunks of cheese, salami, and dark bread spread the kitchen table. I might have been more malleable had I not been raised to dust the stair rail and put the milk away the second after pouring it over raisin bran. I could not live in a pigsty. They couldn't live in a pharmacy.

I would leave and go running to escape the uncomfortable feelings inside. I was grateful Tatyana and Grandma were more than willing to watch the baby. I would leave for the University of Akron, where I'd whittle afternoon hours away in quiet work. "You sure your mother's okay watching Viktor until three?" I leaned against the minivan window. Dima was returning to work at Gotech Electronics, Jerry's company where he had recently begun to work making copies and sales calls or filling boxes in the warehouse with small electronics. He did not complain and worked hard. We continued subtracting from the thousand dollars saved for the visit, and with an unplanned car repair and the mortgage due, there was nothing in the bank. We had hoped he would stay home the whole month, but he had used up all his paid time off.

"She'll be fine," he threw a butter and cheese sandwich on the passenger side seat.

"Listen, be home as soon as possible. I don't know what to do with your parents without you."

"They don't expect to be entertained." His keys rattled in the ignition.

"Sorry you have to go to work." I gathered my things to leave. The book bag twisted around my wrist as I grabbed bottled water, peanut butter bread, and sunglasses, glancing at Grandma's hand-washed housedress sprawled over the kitchen chairs. Somewhere between laughter and irritation, I pressed hard on the gas pedal.

It was nearing dinnertime. I gripped the handle to the refrigerator, sticky. I felt Dima in the room trying to ignore me. "This is disgusting," I whispered as he leaned in for a generic Cola. I smelled

Dove on his clean skin. His family laughed with Viktor Jr. in the living room.

"Dimka! Look, quick. He's crawling for it —" Tatyana was on her full belly holding an empty can of Labatt's. Our son inched over to her, reaching out for the toy. I laughed with the family as my son stared up at me and smiled, as if to ask if this was all right. I gave in to my weary legs and kneeled down behind Tatyana.

"Viktor, come on baby, come on," I coed as he began to crawl.

As easy as it could be to laugh with the family, it was to slide into frustrations, to unleash complaints: your parents need to pick up their messes; we need to communicate who's cooking when; we can't afford all these groceries; when are we going to discuss their not living with us? At the center of it all was Dima. He seemed unwilling to communicate. In the midst of the family's drama, he fell into silence. The family was used to sharing everything, including understanding, and it seemed I was the only dissident among the group. I insisted Dima understand me, but my impatient, emotional persuasions were ineffective.

Dima and I escaped for a quick trip to Marc's for more Labatt Blue. After my laden sighs and tip of the iceberg complaints, he slammed his palms against the steering wheel and screamed. "I can't take this!" I was shaking. This was not the man I had married.

"It's okay," I touched his forearm. "I'm sorry," I said, but he was mute. His face was granite. "Look. Let's pray."

"I can't pray right now," he said.

When the family went shopping that evening, I busted out the rubber gloves. A quick clean. I strapped Viktor into his highchair, glad Tatyana could not see. She would tell Dima we kept the baby too confined again. I wanted to run around the house and restore every room. "Hey, little boy, how are you? Momma loves you," I cooed into his cheek. "Just you and Momma —"

"Momma." I ran to the baby's first year journal wishing Dima was home and resenting that he wasn't. By the time the family returned, I forgot to mention that our baby had said his first word.

The family was happy, drinking and eating a late snack of sour cream and bread and salads. Dima's size-eleven feet flapped over my green flip-flops as he shuffled to the bonfire and stoked the embers. Grandma smiled at me, and warmth spread like wine through my body.

"Grandma wants to make a statement," Dima said. "She said she wants to take care of Viktor in the mornings. That we should put his crib in her room." He turned to her and responded, "Thank you, Grandma. That is a good —"

"Wait. Dima, I'm not comfortable with that. First of all, the computer room is too small for the crib. And, Grandma's not well. She shouldn't have to get up at the crack of dawn with Viktor. You know he's fussy and —"

"Grandma insists," he said.

"No."

"What do you mean? She's doing us a favor?"

"Pleeeese, can we talk about this in private?" His eyes rolled. Silence. I gulped my water and filled the teakettle, re-emerging with notebook and pen.

"Dad says he will volunteer information for your novel," Dima said.

"It's a memoir," I corrected.

"He said when his great-great grandfather gave his daughter away he was afraid she'd come back home to Siberia 'new school.'" His father's pointer finger lingered at the edge of his nostril while he spoke. "In Siberia, people are open, straightforward. If someone's a decent person, they're accepted. If not, the people reject him. See, many criminals sent to Siberia for exile. Dad's friends started getting into trouble when he left for St. Petersburg. He wanted a better life. He was always looking for good people to befriend."

"What did your parents think about you marrying me?" I tried.

"My parents asked me, 'Do you love her?'" he said.

Tatyana interrupted. "Mom says she'd disown me if I married for the wrong reasons." She stared intensely at me when she spoke. "She says American women seek emancipation from men. They want to be independent, do what they wish. Liberal women are ruining the family unit. American women don't think they need a man; they can do everything on their own. But they're separating their lives from their husbands' —" He saw the questioning look on my face and thought an example would make his mother's words clear and accurate. "Mom passed up education for love. She could have gone to university. She's very intelligent, Lea." I'd heard this many times. Tatyana's face looked hard, defensive, but beyond anything, proud.

Breeze rippled over our glasses of wine on the picnic table as Dima's father began speaking. "What did he say?" I asked. Dima entered a long conversation with his father.

"Dad just said he feels bad about being too harsh with me as a child. But I deserved it." I appreciated the way his father could say he was sorry. The family schlepped into the kitchen and piled the sink with teacups. I squirted pink soap on a washcloth. "Grandma's concerned about the color of the soap —"

"What do you mean?" I asked rinsing the dishes.

"She thinks you shouldn't use the dishwashing liquid on the cloth. It might dye it."

As the days bled together, it was more than the flies buzzing through the kitchen with the family's insistence of fresh air, more than their strange icons offered to us as gifts and then taken back to their room. It was the pigeonhole swallowing me, the constant sense that everything was out of my hands. All of life seemed a mere reflection of the family's united will.

Hours before my niece's baptism, Dima and I raged upstairs as I gave Viktor a bath. It was the first time in five years of marriage that the "D" word was uttered. "You're lucky to have me!" I hissed.

"I don't even know who you are," he said.

"You have your citizenship. Go ahead and divorce me. But I get Viktor," I spat through clenched teeth. I had silenced him. He kicked the closet door. No doubt the parents heard that.

"Your parents don't ask. They come into our home and overtake — Viktor, kitchen, you, the whole downstairs! Two women cannot live in the same house together. At least not two strong women like your mother and me!"

"You're so selfish!" he said.

"Why don't you say something else to hurt me? You disgust me—" I said and rinsed the soap from our statue quiet son. As I dried him with a towel, his little hands gripped my shoulders. I carried him to our bed to dress. With each flaming word, burning thought, I wondered if we would ever recover.

I cracked at my niece's baptism. We arrived at Advent Lutheran Church at five. The air was humid, and the church was without air conditioning. The young priest greeted us in a traditional black clergy shirt stuffed into khaki shorts and a multicolored scarf draping his neck. He shook our hands. I looked down at his sandals.

"Pastor Kovlash, Prevet!" he said. The family was silent, unsmiling, as though they hadn't understood his Russian greeting, only slightly mispronounced. It grew unbearably hot. Contemporary Christian music played in the sanctuary.

"Make yourselves at home. You can take Communion. We have open Communion here," Pastor Kovlash ushered us through the doors to the wide sanctuary of plain wood. Nobody made the sign of the cross, bowed, or lit a candle before an icon. The pastor turned to me. "This might be weird if they're Orthodox." Turning to the family, he continued, "Saturday night is our contemporary service. It's all very different Sunday morning." At the front of the sanctuary, a handful of men and women were dressed in jeans and singing off key. Two worship leaders tapped tambourines in front of a black statue frozen in a dance. There were no icons, communal chalice, or incense. The family pressed together in the pew and passed the small plastic cups of grape juice down the row.

"The statue's a demon," Grandma whispered. Tatyana and Viktor were perfectly quiet. Unbreakable. It seemed they didn't consider that the Orthodox Church had symbols of faith that could be misunderstood just as easily by one outside its tradition. Icons, candles, a "showcase" of the church's patron saint appeared distracting for a person used to perceiving Jesus as a friend living inside one's heart through the Holy Spirit. While such perception could seem unclear, it also allowed for a personally contrived vision of God that seemed as familiar as one's self. The family didn't explain the Church, but I wished they would offer a bridge for one unaccustomed to what they found familiar.

We filed into the church and the ceremony proceeded. Dima and I were sponsoring our niece. At the front of the sanctuary, my sister stood in a bright dress holding her child, asleep like a limp doll. Pastor placed an open prayer book in my hands. Dima was mute as I vowed to teach our niece of God. Suddenly, Viktor shrieked in the middle of the ceremony. Tatyana rummaged through the diaper bag looking in vain for a bottle of water. Pastor Kovlash dipped his small hand into the baptismal font and sprinkled my niece's delicate head. Water trickled down her forehead onto the dress with a small pink bow. She didn't stir. Tatyana muffled our son's cries against her bosom and rustled the diaper bag and Grandma from the sanctuary. Viktor and my mother followed them to the lobby. After our vows, Dima and I also slipped from the sanctuary.

"Dima? Where's the water bottle," his mother asked.

I said, "I didn't bring it. The doctor specifically told me to feed Viktor formula if he was thirsty or hungry. These sensations are the same for a baby, and he needs the vitamins in the formula." Grandma pushed her bottom lip even further out from the top and looked crippled with worry. Dima's father drifted to the windows at the side of the lobby.

"The child is thirsty. He needs water." Tatyana said.

"I won't be told how to raise my son. I know what he needs. He's thriving. I've handled it fine this far! Dima, just tell them, tell them what the doctor said."

"Look at him. He's sweating. Aren't you thirsty? Come on!" Dima said. All eyes on the neglectful American wife. I walked away from the bench and Grandma and Tatyana. Dima's father followed me. He put his arm around my shoulders, and I started to cry.

"I am Momma," I sobbed. He chuckled. My mother and Dima followed us outside under the darkening clouds.

"Viktor is thirsty. Think about it. Are you thirsty? I don't know why you're acting like this."

"It is not about the bottle, Dima. Are you listening to me? It's about being told what to do —"

"No one's telling you what to do. They don't understand why the doctor would say that. It doesn't make any sense."

"It doesn't matter if they understand. It only matters that they don't interfere like this when I decide something with our son!"

My mother said, "I understand how you both are looking at things, but listen to me. Your marriage has to be priority. You have to put each other first and work together. Lea, you need to calm down. Dima, your mother needs to back off a little bit." But the conversation ran on and on with no resolution. Dima stared at the cement and I looked at him. Viktor held our son and slowly paced. Us — door — us — door — us. He began to speak.

"Dad said that they are still trying to figure out why Viktor is always in Pampers. He shouldn't have the plastic around his genitals so often or he might become infertile," Dima nodded with his father.

We drifted back into church as it began to rain. Grandma said, "I can tell with the way Lea is acting that when we leave America, we will consider each other enemies." For me, family forgave and accepted each other, but it seemed we were facing an all-together different type of family now. How did unlike cultures reconcile mutual understanding? Growing up, my family forgave as naturally as we were angered. Once, my father slammed the breaks at the end of our street so Mom could exit the minivan and walk to McDonald's instead of coming to church with us after an argument over something as meaningless as feeding the dog. It was only a matter of hours before we were together at Bob Evans after church, laughing and talking easily. On other occasions, we shared conversations on the steps by the kitchen, Mom pausing from the ground meat sizzling in a pan to talk through a disagreement and make my father and me hug before I left the house. I worried Dima's family would remain inflexible and unforgiving.

We were back in the minivan for the short ride to my sister's when Viktor asked, "How old are you?" He craned his thick neck around the passenger seat. His eyes were kind, loving; he had no idea that he'd offended me again.

The breezy dark sluiced the intense day. Family clustered inside the home. My sister, Mom, and Aunt Vicki gathered in the kitchen munching from the veggie tray. "You doing okay, honey?" my aunt asked. I rolled my eyes. "Well, darling, this time too shall pass," she pushed dark hair behind her ears. Viktor Jr. and my sister's little girl squealed in the living room as they circled the coffee table on familiar laps. Dima's family was outside sitting by the pool under an old maple. Tatyana and Grandma were drinking Labatts, and Viktor sipped a glass of red wine. Dima and I flitted around the party.

My family's love warmed me. With the nagging need for resolution, I swigged the water, dropped the broccoli drenched in Ranch dressing, and walked over to Tatyana. She was open to me, and I hugged her, asking her pardon. She hugged me back with strong arms. We loaded into the minivan, finally on our way home for the night, when baby Viktor began to wail. "Dima, stop the car. Deeeem! He's crying," his father pressed. They were not used to Viktor's red faced shrieks, his little body writhing in the car seat.

"I have to pull over, Lea."

"We just need to get home. There's no point stopping. He'll cry again when we start." We stopped. "Whatever," I mumbled unbuckling him. Tall grass tickled my sandled feet at the side of the highway. Viktor fell asleep against the pounding of my heart. "He's sleeping," I whispered and gingerly strapping him into his car seat. Tatyana would not meet my eyes.

We spilled out of the minivan onto the broken driveway. "I'm putting him to sleep," Dima mouthed, shuffling into the house. His family and I stood in the fresh night air, quiet until he rejoined us to translate stories of healing.

"You should walk on the morning dew because it heals blisters. Dad was in the army and had to wear boots for entire days and nights. When his feet became so raw with blisters he could barely walk, someone told him about the cool morning dew. When he began doing this each morning, his feet healed." Maybe it was just the time spent out of the boots, but I was quiet.

Grandma shared a story about her father, who had been an officer in the navy. I had heard of him before, how he was brave and strong. Dima had been afraid of him after dreaming his ghost was chasing him. When he told his mother and Grandma, they took him to his great-grandfather's grave and said he was haunted because he had not said goodbye. After the graveside visit, the spirit didn't return.

Grandma told of her father when he was alive. He was a Communist but he had been sick when a doctor told him to visit an Old Believer, an aged Russian woman said to have healing powers because of her faith in God. Because he was so ill, he was willing to try anything. So he went to the woman who prayed over a dish of holy water and blessed him. She told him to place his arm into the water as she said another blessing over his arm. With this, a long skinny "hair fish" emerged from his arm. He watched as the creature wiggled in the water. As she spoke, she drifted into the distance, slight tremors of emotion rippling her flesh.

We sipped tea and Dima set a plate of stale butter crackers on the kitchen table, ceiling fan humming. "Americans are gluttons — selfish. They only care about themselves," Tatyana began, roaming a hand through her curly hair before reaching for a cracker.

"What does she mean, Dima?"

"They don't care for each other. They don't sacrifice for another person. She's right, woman."

"Does she want to live here?" Could she never move past her prejudice? Or was she reacting defensively to a people she felt excluded from? Was she doing what I often would, seeking the differences that set her apart, unwilling to see ways of coming together? Was she struggling to somehow protect herself from painful change?

"She doesn't know," Dima said.

"My father asks if we'll fight if they live here."

"I don't know," I said. Tatyana began talking, but he didn't translate.

After a time he said, "She just said that she hopes you're not a typical American." Anything seemed easier than living with the parents.

Had I no choice? Was my own life really not my own at all? Maybe infertility had been preparation for the family—to show me how beyond control life really was and to assure me that God gave gifts. Though I believed my family, each member, was a part of that gift — was an opportunity to love — I didn't know if I could find the way to love Dima's parents. What was God allowing, and why did it all seem so intrusive? I had imagined things would be challenging, but why so impossible? Was my faith really so shallow, my love for others so weak that I was breaking already? I wanted to talk but there was silence, and what I did seemed often misunderstood.

I did not want to live with the parents, but decided I would endure with hope that we would come together in time. I was ruining Dima's joy, and I longed to stop self-destructing. I longed for God, our Refuge and Guide, our Comforter. I was desperate to help myself, but the more I tried, the more I knew it wasn't possible on my own.

The family assumed their seats in the van, Grandma up front with Dima, Tatyana and Viktor in the back, baby and I in the middle. We were on our way to visit an Orthodox parish in our neighborhood. It was drizzling, and I wiped the wet from Viktor's hand, savoring his giggle. "We've decided to baptize Viktor in a separate service, not just before Liturgy," Grandma said.

"What? Who's decided? Dima, we don't even have an Orthodox parish we're going to."

"It's okay. That's why we're going to St. Elia the Prophet."

"We don't know that this is the church," I said.

We unloaded from the van and ambled up the cement stairs. The church was old with an iron mesh curling over the entrance. I leaned in for the door as the family backed away and performed a series of bows and crosses, finally entering the sanctuary with their heads covered, eyes to the ground. Viktor told Dima to have me spit my gum. I swallowed it with a gulp, looping my arm through the infant carrier and taking it from Viktor. Sweating, I stooped to the ground just outside the sanctuary and unbundled the baby from the blanket Grandma had wrapped him in.

The parish was small, quiet. Viktor was the only baby. A small circle of faithful sang at the back of the church like delicate bells. The service felt impossibly long and foreign. I took Viktor into the foyer midway through for a bottle and watched the room from a distance. It was not a place I felt able to enter. After Liturgy, the family spoke with the priest — common introductions, the usual story of Dima, hockey, life in the States. Then, to my surprise, Dima told the priest we wanted to baptize Viktor the following week. The priest took our phone number and promised to get back in touch with us to explain a few things.

Once we returned to the van, I derailed the family's plans. I would not baptize Viktor at that church. I had been willing to test the waters of Orthodoxy, but the family would have to be willing to move at my pace. This might have seemed natural to them, the universal Church, but to me it seemed standoffish. If Orthodoxy wasn't an exclusive club for foreigners and their families, if, as writer Frederica Mathewes-Green wrote,[1] the faith was not merely about a philosophy or mystical insight, but was about true events in history that matter for every person everywhere, then I needed to realize a parish had room enough for a young American mother with an Evangelical background.

"Why did we talk to the priest if we aren't going to baptize Viktor there?" Grandma asked, staring out the window with a quivering bottom lip.

"I told you we were rushing this," I mumbled.

I realized that we had a steady balance of two dollars in our bank account while online minutes before leaving for the Upper Peninsula

---

[1] *At the Corner of East and Now*, (New York, Putnam, 2000).

of Michigan. A week with the Holmeses meant gourmet food (and free), nature walks, and another home to fill and undo. I was relieved to be leaving. Grandma entered the computer room.

"Got everything?" I said as she stooped for her plastic bag of clothes. We would drive eight hours there and, as Dima had said "on the way home," (which seemed more out of the way home) we would stop in Chicago to meet an old friend of Grandma's, one of the main selling points in convincing her to return to the States. With the hope of a vacation, I had glossed over the reality of over twenty hours in the van with the family and an eight month-old.

As we backed down the driveway, all seemed happy, despite the humid drizzle. "The family wants to plan a bank robbery," Dima said. "I'll be the driver, Mom and Dad will do the deed, Grandma will scan the scene. Lea, you'll count the money," Tatyana's eyes danced. I laughed with them. After a few hours on the road, we stopped for gas. Tatyana bought a double-scoop pecan ice cream cone and insisted on using her change for Dima's soda too. We stood at the side of the gas station in sticky air. We giggled as Viktor licked the ice cream. I jiggled my legs.

I liked the sound of their Russian and trying to decipher what they talked about. It was like watching a foreign movie. I could sit back from the situation without having to actually participate in it. Tensions mounted, however, as the baby became inconsolable, and we all looked forward to arriving at the Holmes'. They had been around many different kinds of people, and I counted on their worldliness to accept our family. Susan and Jerry didn't let me down, and it was remarkable to experience their patience and goodwill for our family.

"The bathroom smelled like fish because Mom and Grandma didn't know you could flush the toilet paper down the toilet," Dima explained to Susan and me in the kitchen one morning, discussing things. "Grandma's diabetic and can't eat the oatmeal that says 'Quaker' because there's sugar in it —" he continued.

"No. There's less than two grams of sugar. And it's exactly the same as the generic brand she eats every morning," I argued.

"But that one says one gram — look," he pointed to the label. "It's not the same."

I shrugged and continued, "I'm worried about Grandma. She's eating lots of sugar. That ice cream that says 'no sugar added' doesn't mean there's no sugar. There's probably eight grams in one serving, and she's had half the gallon! That's why she has a nose bleed." Susan added blueberries to the Quaker oatmeal and offered to watch Viktor before his afternoon nap. The family finished breakfast and weaved through a slope of pine trees in the backyard to the lake.

"The wet suit fits you well," I told Dima from the dock in my red bikini and dipped a toe in the water. The day was overcast and Lake Huron was cold until late August.

"Come on Dimka! Let's go!" Tatyana plopped on her skidoo. Grandma rode behind Dima in her black bikini, full body partially concealed by the life jacket.

"Whooooho!" His mother cried as they zoomed around the lake. "Now I know how bikers feel!" she laughed.

Viktor slowly waded through the water to a skidoo of his own. "Hey, Dima! Dima! Stay closer! Hey, closer!" He yelled in Russian.

"My Dad's a wimp," Dima whispered as he helped Grandma onto the deck beside me. "Guess what he asked me? He asked if you and I were going into the woods."

"What do you mean?" I asked. He smiled.

That night we crossed the Mackinac Bridge from the Upper Peninsula to the Lower Peninsula and Dima drove the family and Susan into Sault Ste. Marie for all you could eat crab legs. Susan and I squeezed together on the seat next to Viktor. Her hands were tan and her wedding ring sparkled with sunset. Throughout our time Up North, Susan was especially understanding and giving to me, and I rested in our closeness.

Grandma had never tasted crab and was disappointed. She filled up on bread and overdone chicken because the crab meat was "too bland." Tatyana and Viktor laughed, piled their plates with salty crab. There were paintings of nature, rugs, and Native American manikins.

They had silky hair in braids, high cheekbones, and animal hides around their shoulders.

After dinner, Susan gave us twenty dollars each to gamble at the casino in the restaurant. Tatyana and Viktor looked down as Susan zipped her purse. Grandma shook her head and looked in the distance. I smiled at Dima, and he smiled back. We were used to the Holmeses. This kind of generosity didn't surprise us. Susan and I strolled Viktor to the side of the entranceway and fed him a bottle, talking about nothing in particular. Time slipped by as the family laced through the casino.

"Look," Dima pulled the edge of two hundred dollar bills from his khaki pockets. "Dad gave this to me. He felt bad that Susan had to give us money."

"How'd he get money? Thought we were all at nada?"

The next morning, just after six, no one was up. Total peace balanced the needs of the day. God was with us, and I felt His loving-kindness. I ran past tall evergreens on an open road beside the forest. The earth smelled cool and moist. Back at the Holmes', I prayed with my new prayer book, still wondering why one needed to read prayers. I had the urge to call my mother and share peace instead of the frustration she so often heard from me. She would be finishing her first cup of coffee.

She answered on the second ring. "Oh honey! How are you? I've been thinking about all of you. Is Viktor all right?"

"Everything's fine, really. I actually feel so good right now. Everything's going to be all right."

"I know it. I just keep thinking about the way Tatyana and Grandma acted at the baptism. They were so stubborn about feeding Viktor water. What bothered me most was the way they didn't let you have the final say so. They aren't Viktor's mother." I hoped my sister hadn't been bothered. Mom and I continued talking about the prejudice we sensed from Tatyana toward American women and the need for all of us to be willing to change, to learn to accept each other. I wondered about limits to change and acceptance, but was feeling too optimistic to bring anything up that would spiral us both into irresolvable worry.

"I want to do the Lord's will," I began.

"I understand wanting to do what's right, but there need to be limits —"

"Whose, Mom? There's no guidebook here. I'm trying to realize God's will. But, it's the kind of situation that might go a million different ways." While my heart wanted God's will, I was unprepared to do it all at once. It was difficult to realize what amount of giving, relinquishing, and enduring was necessary. Yet, if I chose God, I chose to love them. I knew there was no other way, but learning to step along this narrow way was difficult.

"Me and your Dad are praying for you."

"Thanks, Mom. Do you want to now?" We had never read prayers before. She agreed and I opened the book beside a basket of bananas and peaches.

"O Lord, grant that I may meet all that this coming day brings to me with spiritual tranquility. Grant that I may fully surrender myself to Thy holy Will.

"At every hour of this day, direct and support me in all things. Whatsoever news may reach me in the course of the day, teach me to accept it with a calm soul and the firm conviction that all is subject to Thy holy Will.

"Direct my thoughts and feelings in all my words and actions. In all unexpected occurrences, do not let me forget that all is sent down from Thee.

"Grant that I may deal straightforwardly and wisely with every member of my family, neither embarrassing nor saddening anyone.

"O Lord, grant me the strength to endure the fatigue of the coming day and all the events that take place during it. Direct my will and teach me to pray, to believe, to hope, to be patient, to forgive, and to love. Amen."

"That was really beautiful," she said.

Mr. Holmes made pancakes for breakfast, and the aroma of sweet and coffee filled the room. The family laughed as Viktor sat on a quilt in Jerry's baseball cap and reading glasses. The news broadcasted thunderstorms. Viktor wore a lopsided grin as he reached for the eyeglasses on his head. It would be a day of slow smiles and aimless strolls. A day when Leshiy, the forest devil according to Russian superstition, seemed on the prowl. As the story went, Leshiy had village girls cook for him and in exchange he provided dowries and successful marriages. It was said he could also take women deep into the woods forever.

Later that day as the thunderstorm raged, I called down the street, "Viktor! Viktor! Tatyana? Where are you?" I jogged down the road. Dima had taken a bicycle up and down the island in search of them. Feet squished in the water filling my shoes. What would she do with him in the cold rain? Why would she take him walking when a storm was brewing?

Tatyana appeared in her bra, waving at the edge of the woods. "Lea! Lea!" I sprinted and threw my arms around her. She laughed in my ear and motioned for me to follow her into the forest where her tiger-printed shirt draped our Viktor.

"He's laughing!" I cried holding him to my chest and smoothing his hair. As we walked back to the house in the downpour, I wondered if Dima's father would have a conniption that Viktor Jr.'s hair was wet and uncovered in the cold — surely he'd be sick by morning.

We slipped through the open front door. Susan, Jerry, and Viktor laughed and asked where we'd been. They said Dima was still looking for us. I needed to feel his arms around me. I took our son upstairs and changed our clothes.

Tatyana leaned over the bar in her tiger robe with wet hair in curls around her face. "Dima, Kahlua?" She sounded out the word as he poured it into her coffee. His father was shooting pool.

"Dimka play?" he said. I stood at the side of the room, sipping hot water with lemon. I was at peace watching the family happy.

"Hey, I'll go get your dad and I red wine," I said.

"Nyet! No wine, no water — Leeea need," Tatyana lifted the whiskey bottle. I sat down for a shot. "In English, there's only one way to say things," she began. "The language is nothing like Russian —" She didn't know English. Dima was a man of few words. His translations didn't represent the full English language. I grew faint and dizzy, longing for a bowl of oatmeal and bed.

"Why aren't you eating," Susan asked.

"I don't feel well."

"You should eat a little—" Susan's words pushed through the still room. Tatyana finished and went to bed. Grandma yawned and inched over to the freezer for no-sugar-added ice cream.

"I think there's sugar in that," I said in Russian. But she acted as though she couldn't understand me.

In the morning, Grandma was at the table eating generic oatmeal with olive oil and growling back and forth with Viktor Jr. He screamed, smiling with surprise at the power of his voice. "He's going to wake up Susan," I said, stretching my legs in the living room in front of the news. I walked over to Viktor, whispered, "Shhh, honey, eat your kasha," and kissed his cheek. Grandma grinned, lips crumbled against her gums without the teeth.

I strolled to the end of the driveway with my journal and sat on the warm asphalt. The front door opened and I wondered which of the family was coming. Grandma wore a concerned face as she ambled down the drive in her housedress layered with Dima's sweatshirt. "Lea, Lea!" She continued talking slowly, indecipherably, and pantomiming for me to rise from the ground. The infertility fear. To the side of the drive, she sprinkled corn on the patch of grass where we had seen deer earlier.

"Come on, agent number fifty-seven," Dima called from the house, his father by his side. His father had joked that I was a spy, which was the reason I wrote everything down. "We're going on a 'field trip' with Jerry." Grandma dropped the last of the corn and we walked up the drive together.

Jerry was patient and generous, pointing out the history and culture of the UP and walking the slower pace of the family. He bought us fried fish and filled the silence with careful explanations of tourist attractions. He didn't seem to mind Grandma pulling money from her bra, or the photographs taken at every stop, or the silence he graciously broke. "Dad's more easygoing," Jerry told me as we walked ahead of the family to the minivan.

We were leaving for Chicago the following morning to visit Grandma's childhood friend. He was a Jew and had immigrated to the States on a religious asylum passport twenty years earlier. Despite distance and time, Grandma and the man connected all these years later simply because they had once been friends in Russia. The day was endless before the release of night. Susan had been especially kind with me — understanding smiles, questions in soft tones. She seemed to sense my need to walk the island. "I'm going to the store. Vegetable soup's on the stove." I thanked her from the computer, tucked to the side of the pool table, where I was emailing a friend from New Grace. Dima and his father played pool.

I could not explain the change in my faith, though I tried. Orthodoxy appealed to me on an intellectual level, but it also seemed to inform a transitioning way of life that would be the way to become a healthy, happy family. The Faith was a way of life that mended and healed from the soul outward. I thought the fifth-century abbot, St. John Climacus', notion of joyful sorrow[2], where repenting and rejoicing was the basis of Orthodox spirituality, extended the I-have-a-friend-in-Jesus attitude. Because we could be close with Christ through the holy sacraments and Tradition of the Church, there was joy, and there was sorrow for sin that separated one from God. It was more realistic to allow sorrowful emotions (than to stifle them as in some Protestant communities I'd been a part of), and infinitely good to realign one's feelings with God. Furthermore, facing one's emotions was central to realizing sin. It was important to pray that thoughts and feelings be guided by the Holy Spirit. Acknowledging what was inside was oftentimes a step towards change that would reconcile one to God and others. Being a Christian began with my own heart and mind, but it didn't stop there. It was always about relation-

---

[2] *The Ladder of Divine Ascent,* trans. Colm Luibheid and Norman Russell, (New York: Paulist Press, 1982).

ships with others from my own relationship with God. Unable to explain the spiritual changes happening within me, I offered my friend titles of Orthodox books to read.

Dima and his father set the pool sticks down, and his mother and Grandma followed from behind the bar as we gathered around the table for a late lunch. The room had large panels of windows and the sunlight was warm. "My mom said she's going to put three hundred in our account," I told Dima. He shook his head and looked down. We were desperate for intimacy. "But you still need to go into work. We can't survive without income —"

"I know that," he said looking up with a steely gaze.

"But I still don't know why you would think we could get by if you didn't work while your family is here."

"I wasn't thinking, okay?" Grandma looked at the soup, under bite quivering, and I suddenly felt remorse.

"Can we say a prayer?" I asked. His father said something and rose from the table.

"Dad says he'll say one." His father returned to the table with a rule of prayer in Russian. We crossed ourselves and Viktor mumbled an indiscernible strand of words. The family crossed themselves, and I followed.

"Thanks," I said, looking away from his father with tears in my eyes. I blew on the soup and steam eased tension in my face. After eating, Grandma excused herself to her room. Dima and I and his parents strolled Viktor to the marsh at the end of the island. Birds called and breeze rustled through cattails. We stopped suddenly and Dima turned to his mother. She cried against his shoulder as he said, "Mom doesn't want to burden us. Tough times can strengthen our relationship, but if they last too long they will destroy us." He rubbed his mother's back.

"Tell her we won't be destroyed. We have a strong relationship. We always have," I softly said.

"She feels awful that they can't help us more financially."

"Baby, I don't care about that. Money is the least of it for me. I just don't want to live together forever," or even temporarily. He didn't translate. In the silence, I sensed God wanted me to be open to the possibility. How could I deny them a home and their son? No one would take my son from me. How could Christ die? How could we deserve such mercy and love?

"Tell your mother I like the sound of her voice. It's strong and sexy." She smiled and we kept walking, my arm strewn through his father's, hers through Dima's as he pushed the stroller.

Later that night, Dima called from the hallway where he sifted through a box for beach shoes. "Hey, we're going down to the dock, riding the skidoos one more time!" I looked up from the bowl of cherries, which I had been biting in half and sharing with Viktor. I guessed the family assumed I'd be babysitting. Dima's mother trailed him in her bathing suit with Viktor's sandals flapping from her feet. I chewed the cherry half slowly. It was a calm evening, only an hour or so left before the dark would settle in and we'd have to dock the skidoos. Susan turned from the sink.

"Why don't you go with them? I'll watch Viktor for a bit." I agreed, kissed Viktor's cheek, and slid into the six dollar flip flops Susan had bought me at the grocery store.

I didn't have my bathing suit on and still wasn't sure about getting in the frigid water, but it would be a shame not to ride the skidoo once. "Lea, there's room on the back of mine," Mr. Holmes said, scooting forward on the skidoo. "Here," he waded through the water to the dock and piggybacked me to his skidoo. "Ready?" We flew over glass-like water as the sun set. The wind pushed my face, carried my screams into the open air. I squeezed my arms around Jerry's middle as he pushed the machine as fast as it would go into the center of Lake Huron. Small waves knocked under us. He circled around to ride our wake, swelling and crashing. The shoreline looked even against the dark forest. I wondered where life would take us as my body tensed behind Jerry. Lord have mercy.

It was nine that night. Way too late for salmon. I picked at nuts in the kitchen with Susan, trying to piece together the next part of our journey even though by then I knew better than to try and plan things out with the family. The strategy was to leave before dawn so Viktor could sleep hours of our trip away, but I thought we'd be lucky to leave by eight or nine.

"So tell me about your new church," Susan said. We had always talked freely about God, but recently our conversations had been muted.

"There's a lot of stuff I'm trying to figure out. What do you want to talk about?" I asked.

She said, "I think when people grow more mature with their faith they want a more traditional church. I know you take your faith seriously." She paused. "There are two problems I have with the Orthodox Church. Praying to the saints and closed Communion. What's the point in praying for people who have died?" She filled the pan with water, plunked in the corn on the cob.

"I really hope I don't misspeak. It's confusing for me, too, Susan. But the Church says there's one heavenly kingdom, including those alive in the Faith and those who have fallen asleep in the Faith. When we pray, we ask God for mercy for those we love if they are here or asleep in the Lord."

"But what difference would it make if you pray for those who've already died? We can't change their free will. They either chose God or rejected Him," she said.

"If our prayers affect people on earth, maybe they also affect those not here with us." By God's infinite love our souls were immortal, and even on earth the Holy Spirit abided in those being saved to experience this eternal presence of God's love. In the Kingdom, God's love was full—and, depending on one's heart, would be an experience of bliss or hell. Humanity and God cooperated in prayer. Praying for others was the ultimate act of love, which had no limits, not even time or place, not even death.

"Don't you think it is every individual's right to take Communion? No one has a right to judge another person's heart," she said. I agreed that it was every individual's right to take Communion. Christ wanted all people to come to him. Tragically, not everyone chose the

Lord. If a person refused Him, he could not partake of the body and blood of God. In Orthodoxy, the priest prayed Christ mystically become the bread and wine. It was not a rational translation of body and blood but a miracle. Before drinking the blood and eating the body of Christ, the priest prayed that we become His nature and He become ours. It seemed if a person didn't confess belief in this experience, he wouldn't desire participation with those who did. Truth would never be compromised, and this could seem offensive. Holy Communion was unity with each who partook in Christ. This differed from Protestant traditions where the body was symbolized in bread, the blood in grape juice (or wine). The experience of Communion was not literal unity in Protestantism, but it was in the ancient tradition of the Church.

Communion was for everyone in the Faith. The Faith was the Church, was obedience to the Body of Christ, despite how one felt, or what happened in life, or how much or little one understood in a particular time and place. Becoming a Christian was an unending search for life in Christ and the simultaneous choice to believe by faith. It was about acting on that choice, from a place of faith—no matter how weak or small.

## CHAPTER THIRTEEN

# Emptying Our Nest

The morning unfolded easier than I had dared imagine. Aside from Tatyana losing her roll of film, Dima spilling a cup of coffee, and Viktor refusing to settle in the car seat, the morning had come and gone. We were back in the Povozhaev Express and off to Chicago, loaded with crackers and smoked whitefish spread that Susan had care packaged. "Grandma's diabetes," the family insisted when they opened the fish at ten in the morning. I hoped Dima would speed just a little.

We did not know where we'd be sleeping that night. Grandma had called her childhood friend a handful of times, but, in typical Russian style, the plans would be relayed once we were there. Grandma and Dima chatted at the front of the van, WWII stories, and Viktor and Tatyana napped in the back. I wrote in my journal and read, groggy but too uncomfortable for sleep, body stiff, mind abuzz. I wondered about the family we would stay with. It was odd to be traveling hours to stay with strangers — but, then again, I thought of Dima's parents and Grandma traveling to the States to stay with us.

Grandma's friend met us at the corner of his Chicago neighborhood in a Lexus. Dima and I greeted him first. He was small and excited. "I pay eighty-thousand dollars for car," he told me as we walked around his vehicle and back into the borrowed minivan to follow him home. He didn't seem humble like Grandma, and I had concerns about the families relating to one another. He helped Grandma from the van and kissed her hand. They embraced, both weeping. Their home was clean and light with gold and black décor, outdated modern in the style of the early 1990s. There was a bowl of sparkly fruit in the center of the glass table and a zebra-patterned rug beneath. Glossy pictures of the family with tremendous hairdos covered a wall.

"He play?" the man's wife asked, pointing to a stuffed lion the size of the baby.

"Ah, he's still too small. But thank you." I smiled and held Viktor tight to stop his squirming. I helped the woman spread a tablecloth and set china. She trembled. She spoke in a husky, accented voice and told how her family had come from St. Petersburg to Chicago a generation ago.

"Can I help you with the food?" I asked. She motioned for me to follow her into the kitchen. It was easy to play daughter with her on this temporary basis. We began a strange version of Thanksgiving dinner: cold slices of turkey and cranberry sauce, crab salad, smoked salmon on rye bread, breaded cauliflower, caviar, and blackberry wine. We had just sat down and sipped the warm wine when Viktor Jr. fussed. Dima and his mother and I set up a port-a-crib and tried to calm him to sleep, to no avail.

"Here. Put him in here," Dima said patting the crib.

"He's not going to sleep. This place is foreign to him," I said.

"Dima? Come eat!" Grandma's friend called in a booming voice. The three of us rejoined the party. Tatyana reached for Viktor, but he cried for me.

"Lea, eat?" Grandma's friend asked.

"Okay." I hid behind the baby and shoveled dark bread and salmon into my mouth while Russian animated the table. Viktor wouldn't stop fussing.

"I'm going to take him down the street," I whispered to Dima. The table quieted. "Ah, I'll be right back," I slipped away before the general consensus was pronounced. Dima's mother followed me out the front door. We crawled down the street, Viktor in my arms. The air was still and locusts buzzed in the trees.

"Bugz," said Tatyana.

"Do you like Chicago and Grandma's friends?" I asked in Russian.

"I like Adaline Drive," she said in English.

"I think it's lovely here," I said with thoughts of public transportation, Russian community, and a bit of distance for all of us to adjust to their eventual stay.

That night, the Chicago family offered to pay for Dima, me and Viktor to stay in a hotel room. Tatyana looked down, and I knew she wanted to stay with us. She whispered to Dima, but he told her we needed time alone, and she let it go completely.

"My parents have to live in Chicago when they come," Dima said as we fell against the cool comforter on the hotel bed. "I'll tell them. There's much more opportunity for them here."

"Just make sure you explain exactly what you mean." We seemed to mutually understand and the words would only clutter our joy in being alone together this night. "I really think your mother wants to live with us."

"No. She understands everything."

"You keep saying that, but I don't get that impression at all." He rolled over and wrapped me in his arms.

"This hotel room is a total Godsend," he said.

"No kidding. Your mother wanted to come —"

"That's only because she felt uncomfortable staying with people she doesn't know. She's a shy person," he said. Viktor was silent in the crib at the end of our bed.

"I'll go to the bar —" he said.

"With what money? Look, buy the cheapest red wine they've got." I peeled the banana from the doggie bag the Russians had insisted we take, after carrying our bags to the hotel room, which they had paid for. So much generosity in our lives. I gulped down the banana and rubbed my aching stomach as Dima returned with glasses of Merlot. A half smile pulled at the corner of his lips.

The next morning, the families called Dima's cell phone over breakfast to announce the day's plan and he took the call into the lobby. I unwrapped the silverware and leaned down to Viktor in his umbrella stroller. I jiggled a spoon to distract him from wiggling in the stroller.

"What did they say?" I paused from my egg sandwich as Dima approached the table.

"They've decided I should watch Viktor and you should go with Grandma's friends to sightsee city."

"What? Who decided? Why would they think that?" I gulped the coffee. "No way—"

"Calm down, I already told them that just the three of us are going downtown," he said with a sly smile.

We took the L into downtown Chicago and walked for hours, strolling Viktor through Millenium Park and along the Navy Pier and finally down the Magnificent Mile, eight blocks of shopping along North Michigan Avenue. We passed expensive souvenir shops and restaurants and, finally, couldn't not stop. "Let's just get an appetizer and share it?" I decided. Because Dima was always lunging for a chance to go out to eat, we had silently agreed that I had to be the one to break down. We stepped into an Oriental restaurant and parked Viktor's stroller at a back booth. After small meals and Cokes, we left for our hotel.

Our time in Chicago was fleeting. For the first time in weeks, we spent two nights separated from the family. It renewed us. Grandma's friend's son invited us to a cookout—steak and slushy Heineken from an ice-packed cooler. The family owned a diamond company. The home was luxurious with granite tabletops and china in a buffet (though we used paper plates "American" style). The four-story home was as clean as typical in America. Their style was Russian, outdated modern, but blended with real hardwood floors and leather furniture, big screen televisions and classical paintings. The young wife took us on a tour, mentioning they would be adding a Jacuzzi and sauna to the back of the house.

Tatyana seemed impressed, "Like this?" she asked. I nodded but guarded against wanting material things that I knew from experience wouldn't really satisfy the need for love, joy, peace, and purpose.

Grandma's friend's son said that they could live again in Russia if they had to. He said they could return to the dormitories, where I had lived while studying in Nizhny Novgorod. I wondered how a family with two boys could live in a one room dormitory, but he seemed to want to make clear that he knew the transience of having.

When we left Chicago, Grandma's friends gave us gifts: Chicago T-shirts, the stuffed lion for Viktor, and two-dollar bills. A bag of food had been prepared for Grandma, and contact information had been exchanged between the friends. I couldn't believe how well the family cared for us, though they hardly knew us. I sensed what Dima meant about hospitality Russian style versus American.

As Dima maneuvered the Povozhaev Express along another endless highway, we rested in the minivan. His mother leaned against the window, and his father snored softly against her shoulder. Grandma seemed lost in memories. I felt ready to take on the last of the visit — maybe cook a bit more, definitely try to be more patient. I considered making the Thanksgiving turkey Dima had wanted.

"Dima, ask your family if they're glad to be going back to our house," I said.

"You can say that." He wore my sunglasses, too small black ovals reflecting in the rearview mirror. Tatyana exhaled deeply and leaned forward with an empty plastic bottle to give to our son as a toy. Dima said his mother thought Chicago was nice, but it was difficult to stay with people she didn't know. I guessed that meant she knew me.

"But they received us better than my own brother does," his father said with a groggy voice, bunching the pink jacket from Salvation Army behind his back. Grandma silently sat in the passenger seat.

"Grandma, do you feel all right?" I asked. She shook her profile and pointed to her swollen ankles.

"Grandma needs to eat. Bust open the cooler," Dima ordered. I rummaged through my purse for hand sanitizer and offered some to the family. Viktor hesitated and said, "little bit." Grandma shook her head.

"Explain to Grandma that Purell is safe, honey. It's good to kill the junk on our hands —"

"We don't know what's in that stuff. I'm not so sure —"

"Do not be ridiculous, Dima!" I snapped the bottle closed and tore a handful of dark bread from our loaf. "Here, Grandma." Tatyana passed watermelon to me.

"In Russia," Grandma began, "people can't sell their potatoes without paying foreigners from the Caucasus Mountains. And if we don't pay the foreigners, they pour gasoline over our produce." She shook her head.

"If I were back home, I wouldn't let anyone do that to you. Where's the respect for the elderly?" Dima said.

His mother nodded vigorously and began a long tirade about youth and their disrespect. She concluded, "You cannot imagine how things have changed in Russia. Young people want to be like the West."

We rolled up our driveway by ten that night. By eleven, after a solid hour of our baby's screaming, "Viktor's asleep," I whispered to the family, reemerging in the kitchen where they snacked on cheese, shrimp, and tea.

"What's all this?" I asked Dima.

"We didn't have anything else to eat." I rolled my eyes.

New dishes added to the week old ones in the sink; bags, suitcases, and dirty clothes spread over the living room, kitchen, and trailed to their rooms. We had forgotten to feed the cat and she retaliated by spitting clumps of black and white fur over the carpet.

"What are you doing?" Dima's voice cut through my fury into the computer room for the vacuum. I wouldn't look at him.

"This is totally ridiculous! It's going on midnight," he said.

"Dima, I am vacuuming. This place has become a complete pigsty. I can't live like this — I just can't."

"You can't vacuum; Viktor just fell asleep. You'll wake him up. Think about it." The family was quiet in the kitchen.

"Let's take this outside," I said, filling a plastic cup with cold water. The screen door slammed.

"You're acting crazy," he began.

"I'll tell you what's crazy! This situation is crazy! I don't care, Dima, I can't do this. You are totally impossible with your parents here. You act like you haven't lived in America the past fourteen years. What's happened to you?" I could not stop, did not try to stop. I felt like a yoyo unraveling.

"I've not cleaned the entire house since they came, but there's cat hair everywhere, and Viktor crawls on the floor, and I can't sleep with boxes unpacked let alone the tornado of crap we have in there now!"

"They can hear us," he said.

"I don't care!" I threw the cup of water at him. He silently turned from me, the keys jiggling in his hand, and walked to the van.

"Where are you going?" I asked. No answer. "Dima, where are you going?" The engine turned. Exhaust spewed. Tires rolled backward, and he turned down the street. I stormed past our driveway and into the night in the opposite direction.

The stars were bright. "God, what do I do? With everything in me, I do not want them to live with us. What are you asking of me? How can we handle this? Oh God, help me!" I continued around the block, the usual calm from physical release barely making an inroad. I thought about going to my mother's, but this was my life. I knew my mother would never sleep, never relax if she knew what we were going through — the extent of it. I told myself not to do it, not to call her and complain the way I thought I always would. I knew there had to be a better way. "God help me!"

There was nowhere to go but home. Shaky with nerves and hunger, I pulled raisin bran from the shelf and slumped over the table. Viktor turned the teakettle off and filled his mug, sitting down at the table with me. Suddenly, it was all too much. My anger broke as tears dripped into the cereal.

"Viktor, I'm sorry. I—I. This is just hard. I love you. It's just—" I did not know what it was. He was silent, stared ahead, sipped tea. I lost my appetite and went upstairs.

Dima returned and he and his father were in the kitchen talking. I was reading in our bedroom, waiting, when he slipped his leg against mine under the sheet. My anger was dormant with the heat of his body and generous silence. He had gone to the gas station, he said. His voice was deep and soft as he told me what his father had said.

"He asked if you were a jealous person. They think you're acting like this to let us know they can't live with you. My parents don't want to put pressure on me. But you and I and Viktor are their best shot at a functional family. Their parents are elderly; my uncle's an alcoholic. They have no one else."

"I'm not jealous." I turned off the light, set the book behind the bed, and curled on my side. I expected he would grab the pillow and stomp to the couch, but I couldn't respond. Didn't trust myself to. Numb.

His hand brushed my back. "It's going to be all right," he said. "I don't know how. But it is. Orthodoxy will connect the dots in our family."

"How in the world is that possible? I don't see the connection."

"I just have faith," he breathed.

We worried about Grandma. The nose bleeds didn't stop, and her entire leg swelled to twice its normal size. She began to go to sleep earlier and stay in bed longer. I held Viktor on the side of our house, breathing in the fresh summer night and calming us to sleep. Grandma shambled onto the driveway with a cup of water. She grinned, barely meeting my eyes, and dipped her fingers into the plastic cup. She sprinkled the baby's hair, my hair, and made the sign of a cross over us. She hobbled up the chipped cement step to the side door, not saying a word, crossed herself and splashed water over the door handle. Soon she was back in bed, this time moaning with fever. I signed a cross over her bare back. She gripped the sheet and pulled it over her.

Grandma stopped wearing dentures and combing her hair. Her cane was a feeble aid as she inched from place to place. "I understand Grandma can't help it," I said to Dima one morning, "but it's your job to clean their bathroom." My voice was calm, resolved.

"I understand. It's bad. I'll do it," he said.

The vacuum roared under the kitchen table and chairs as the parents and Grandma shuffled new bags into their bedrooms filled with "deals" from another bout of shopping—another winter coat from the Salvation Army, extra-wide shoes for Grandma, a fake spider on clearance. I stopped the vacuum, nudging the cat away from my leg.

"Does your mother think I'm crazy?" He leaned over the kitchen table, arranging tea cups.

"She said everyone has his or her quirks." I stared at his back. "She's asking you to please not clean until they arrive back home once they leave."

"Why? What do you mean?"

"In Russia it's bad omen to clean before guests arrive home. I know you won't believe this, but it's for real." The plane flight alone was twelve hours. My grip on the vacuum handle tightened.

Tatyana sat at the kitchen table with Dima one morning. Her voice trilled in the breakfast nook, and I felt light, happy. I chopped onions for a roast, tears streaming from my eyes. They were leaving in a week and a half, and we all seemed ready for the return to normalcy, all but Dima's father. His sighs were almost unbearable.

"Everything's such a big deal," had become Dima's running complaint.

Some of his mother's resentment towards Americans, particularly women, seemed to come from an inner frustration with America's inaccessibility. She wanted conversation. She wanted familiarity with everything from the temperature of the freezer to what could be purchased at Marc's. She wanted to busy her hands in a kitchen of her own. I started to see her devotion to the family.

"Mom, you were a very good mother," Dima told her. "You had to work, but that was fine. I'm glad I learned how to take care of myself," he said. She shut her eyes as he embraced her, the morning sun filling the breakfast nook.

Viktor came into the kitchen with Viktor Jr. clinging to his bare shoulder. Sigh. "Remember when your uncle forgot you at the beer kiosk?" he asked Dima. He shook his head and seemed to regret the moment his father had interrupted.

"You were only three. My brother took you into the city and forgot about you after a few beers!" Viktor chuckled. "A lady found you near the kiosk and asked where you lived. You said you didn't know the name of the street or city, but you showed her where to take you home."

"Actually, I sort of remember that now," he said.

"The onions burn Lea's eyes because she doesn't cook enough," Tatyana said, half smiling. I rinsed the knife and my hands, smiling back at Tatyana. Despite the peaceful morning together, I couldn't stop worrying about Grandma and wondered why Dima's parents seemed to treat her lethargy as a matter of course. Maybe it was only a matter of wanting to go home. Maybe they were used to diabetes affecting Grandma, but she had been in bed for days and emerged only for meals and tea, usually without a word and for the least amount of time possible.

"Is Grandma depressed or sick?" I asked. Tatyana and Viktor said this was normal, that Grandma would eat too much sugar and then have to rest. They quieted their concern, knowing there was little to be done until they returned home with Grandma.

She suffered quietly with low moans mumbled into the pillow. "Grandma, are you all right?" Her lip folded between her gums, eyes focused. She endured in a trained way. Nonetheless, suffering was a collective experience — for Russians and Americans. We ached together as Grandma's condition became serious.

The dinner roast was dry, the onions and garlic potent. Dima's father was the first to crack a joke, breathing like a dragon and slicing off the top of the peppered meat. Dima asked where I came up with this recipe, and I tried to explain that I hadn't realized the meat was already seasoned and had added pepper.

Cooler air had finally replaced the humidity, and it felt pleasant outside at the picnic table. Everyone seemed eager to give a smile or offer a story. Grandma sipped tea and gummed dry toast. Dima translated her story. "Russians are loyal people. In WWI, we marched to the Winter Palace in the middle of St. Petersburg with posters and icons to beg for help from the tsar. 'He's not home,' the guards said, but the people didn't believe them and demanded to see the tsar.

"The guards opened fire on the people, but the people refused to leave and instead pleaded for mercy. This became Bloody Sunday."

*Emptying Our Nest* 157

Grandma shook her head and winced, placing a hand on her crimson knee.

"Today's young Russians are dishonoring their families and all that was done for them. They are ignoring their Orthodox heritage," she continued. I felt grateful the family encouraged Dima to remember his people's history and faith. Orthodoxy was central to a way of life in Russia, and I wondered how it would affect our lives in America.

Viktor asked me about the semester I'd spent in their homeland six years ago. "How did you perceive people in Russia?"

"The older people seemed quiet, introverted, and unfriendly. The younger people seemed interested in me and in America," I said.

Viktor nodded with understanding. "The older generation was brainwashed to believe America was responsible for the problems in Russia. When I was in the army, there were posters with American soldiers that said 'number one enemy.' The people were told that poverty and problems in the government were all on account of the U.S. I didn't believe the propaganda because it was stereotypical. Why would simple folk, like an American farmer, care about destroying a simple Russian farmer? I believed there were simple people everywhere, and I couldn't believe that all Americans were bad." Were people he might not consider simple somehow bad?

The next afternoon, the friend from New Grace I had emailed Up North called. "I've been thinking about you," she began. I slipped sandals on and stepped through the side door. Our roses had shriveled and drooped at the side of the home. "How are things with church?" she asked.

"Good. It's foreign still, but I feel drawn to the Orthodox Church. I just keep going back to the fact that it hasn't splintered to different denominations."

"Just make sure you're not worshipping man. It's all about Jesus and a personal relationship with Him," she said.

"Absolutely. The Church actually came before the Bible, and the body of believers, through His Church, is undivided!" She was silent. "Why would our individual interpretations of the Bible be more credible than the Church Fathers' that have been passed through the ages? Don't you think we should pay attention to the two thousand years of Christian history?"

"You need to be careful, Lea, and keep praying about it. Ask Jesus to guide you," her voice was flat. I tore a cluster of brittle roses from the bush and threw them to the ground. When we hung up, I was heavy. I hated disconnecting from other believers. I knew it wasn't supposed to be this way. Our personal relationship with Jesus Christ united us also to one another. It was always about Him, and in the reality of our relationships with others His love and our faith was made manifest. I couldn't deny what I began to believe: If the Church was the body and blood of the Lord, its nature had not changed. What had been, remained what was, and what would always be. The faith was timeless and universal. Truth couldn't be denied, no matter how high the cost.

After our visit to St. Elia the Prophet, the family remained silent concerning Viktor's baptism. The issue pressed me. It was important to them, and before they left it seemed my responsibility to concoct a plan with all in agreement. I called Fr. Andrew and let him know Dima's parents and mine planned to attend Liturgy that Sunday with us. He said we would talk with him after service.

That Sunday, the church didn't feel exclusively foreign with the Georgeses and my family and many others who appeared American. Father had told me that many in the parish were Greek, Russian, Romanian, but many were also American converts from Protestantism. The mix of peoples gave the distinct impression that the past and present, the East and West were gathered together to worship the Lord. Though there was still the unusual crossing and chanting, incense and icons, many people smiled and talked with us before and after Liturgy, and they seemed accessible to me, Dima, and our parents. Overall, the people there were less concerned about appearing Christian and seemed more natural. There were still many things that were foreign to what church had been for the past twenty-six years, including the scent of incense, crossing, bowing, and icons. These seemed a part of others' traditions, and I wondered how to enter in. Again I wondered what it meant to be a Christian, willing to change more than before.

My mother and I slipped from the sanctuary with the baby fussing. She seemed slower than usual as we passed Viktor between us in the lobby. Though she never wore much makeup, this morning she didn't have any on. She looked older.

"Are you okay, Mom?"

"I'm all right, just not feeling happy. Your father and I have little in common," she looked away. They must have fought on the way to church, probably over coming to St. Nicholas. They had been visiting the Lutheran church down the street from my sister, and Mom was hesitant to leave my sister and her family for yet another church. They weren't sure what to expect from church anymore. Dad wanted to go to the Georges' church. Orthodoxy was his last stop, he said.

"I'm all right," she said again.

"No. Talk to me."

"I just think every church is the hardest thing. Not one will be perfect. We have to just love Jesus and each other. I don't know." I didn't know what to say to her, but I believed there was more to the Christian life and that God was leading us.

"I really like Fr. Andrew. He is honest, open, and clear —" Viktor squirmed in my arms. "Let's try to go back in the sanctuary. With luck, he'll be quiet." I looked down at the baby. I didn't want to talk. We were there to experience the mystery, and the atmosphere there helped one let go of thinking and simply be.

The church was bright and icons spanned the walls and ceiling. The Georgeses explained that icons were like pictures of loved ones who had passed away. They said the depictions were not idols but loved as representing loved ones. They were windows into the heavenly. While I tried to see this in the somber faces of Christ, I felt little. They weren't familiar. They weren't depictions of what I had always imagined Christ looked like. Yet, unlike some of my Protestant family and friends who found the icons offensive and even insulting, they didn't strike me in this way either. I felt I should be reverent of them somehow, and even believed I would be in time.

After service, Peter Georges hugged me. I asked for his prayers for the family. He and my parents talked until Fr. Andrew quickly slipped into the pew in front of my family and Dima's. He shook Dima's hand, then mine, saying he felt we already knew each other from earlier phone conversations. Viktor extended his arm and bowed. His mother stood as unflinching as a pillar. Grandma's back pushed straight against the pew.

Dima explained, "Father, we want to baptize Viktor next weekend. My family is returning to St. Petersburg, and they want to see him enter the Church." The priest's dark hair was parted down the middle, bangs carefully in place above intense eyes. He listened without interrupting. He seemed completely concentrated, though his face did not display what he felt or thought. He turned to me.

"Lea, how do you feel?" Gratitude swelled.

"Confused," I wept. "And I think we need to let our journey into Orthodoxy 'ferment,' as you had mentioned to me on the phone—" I lowered my eyes from his, studied the bluish veins rising on the back of my hand. I was strangely hesitant in the face of the family's insistence that we save our son's soul without delay. "I know Dima and his family want the baptism now. But I want us to be baptized as a family, and I don't know if I'm ready. I'm trying to understand," I felt like a glass jar slowly cracking. Tatyana's eyes didn't waver from the icons at the front of the church. "I think we should wait," I finished, biting my cheek.

"When do you see Viktor being baptized?" Father asked.

"Christmastime," I said without a thought.

After church, we drove to my aunt's house. The atmosphere in the minivan felt plastic.

"Make a list of Russian words, so I can talk to them," Aunt Vicki had said weeks before. Grandma and Tatyana were exchanging looks at the table where Dima and I, my mother, father, aunt, and Melanie and her family nibbled nuts and tortilla chips. Tatyana's round shoulders were pushed back, and she and Grandma offered no smiles or attempts at communicating with my family. After a string of fast syllables and Tatyana shaking her head, I asked Dima, "What, exactly, are they talking about?" I knew it was about the baby. About something I was doing wrong.

As he hesitated, my heart raced. In a monotone voice he said, "They're talking about Viktor and why he isn't clapping yet. They think he's developmentally behind because he's not stimulated enough." Fluid, unthinking, I scooped Viktor off the floor and walked out the front door. Viktor had said his first word, was making all sorts of word-like sounds, was crawling like a pro, standing up and nearly walking — developmentally behind ridiculous Russian ideas!

The sun pierced the day like fire searing the top of my head. Barefoot, I tread past square lawns and uniform houses, breathing in the heat. I rubbed Viktor's tiny back with icy hands. "Strength, dear God, to deal with the family." I made it half way around the block and turned back for my aunt's. There was no point running away, and I felt calmer. I decided to tell them myself. We could not live together.

Tatyana, Viktor, and Dima lined the garage door as though a unified front. I wondered where Grandma was as my steps quickened. I didn't feel embarrassed but resolute. We all had to try. We all had to change. I walked up to them and looked Dima and then his parents in the eyes. "I understand that your parents love us. But you need to translate this. I don't care that it is going to be very difficult to say. You can blame it on me, I don't care." He nodded. "I do not want them living with us when they move here. There will be many occasions when we don't understand each other. Many episodes when we feel angry and confused. We need time to adjust without the added pressure of living together. They need to adjust to the culture without living under our roof." I stared straight into Tatyana's dark eyes. She stared back without flinching.

After Dima translated, his father quickly said, "We never planned on living with you." He paused and Tatyana spoke quickly.

I studied her face as Dima relayed her words. "When we were growing up, I didn't believe what elders told me. I didn't think they understood me, or my situations. I would only pretend to listen, but secretly I decided to do things my way. Now I see what my elders had said is true. Now, I understand." She laughed; perhaps this new perspective satisfied her. But I saw it differently.

"Yes, we are young. But there are cultural differences that you have to adjust to. Do you want to move here, to be with us?" No answer.

Dima said, "Stop bringing up 'cultural differences.' They will learn English —"

"I realize you did. But you were thirteen. It's got to be harder for them, and impossible if your mother doesn't want to. And Dima, it's not just the language I'm talking about." I couldn't begin to name all that was implied: from family expectations to social conditions, from eating habits to spending tendencies, from friendships to womanhood in America — everything. It was too early and maybe altogether impossible to explain. While mutual understanding may not have been possible, we needed a larger margin of acceptance and tolerance of each other's differences.

His father had one predominant concern. "Are you going to let my dad coach Viktor in hockey?" His father's smirk was easy to forgive, his green eyes soft and glassy. I laughed.

"Of course."

"But will you be watching over his shoulder?" I stared at Dima's father.

"Of course," I said. His smile dropped and he shook his head. He and Tatyana spoke at once, and Dima had to slow them down and translate in his condensed way.

"They are concerned this fight will upset our relationship."

"Dima, you have to explain how it is in my family. We fight and make up. There won't be any grudges on my part. I'll have a harder time if we don't talk, if we don't get out what's bothering us. Then I'll obsess with the what-ifs and the problems will grow." Under the shade of my aunt's garage, we had become a triangle — Dima and his parents facing me. We fell into a circle as Viktor threw his arm around Tatyana and squeezed Dima's shoulder. I held the baby in the center of us.

My aunt's house was silent. Grandma sat at the dining room table weeping and blowing her nose in an old kerchief. The dog licked her swollen toes, until I moved it away and kneeled before her. "Please, forgive me." I reached for her hand, but she shooed me away with her kerchief and wouldn't look at me, chin quivering, thick spectacles in her hand. On rubbery legs I scooped the shrimp stir-fry, my mother rubbing my back. My greatest hope was for Dima to understand, to love me enough.

Back home again, Dima and I put Viktor down for a late afternoon nap. We huddled together over the baby, and I whispered, "Are you disappointed with me?"

"No."

"He's sleeping. Let's go for a walk. Alone," I said. The air was sweet with cherry blossoms. "What's your problem? I can't stand it when you're totally mute."

"I'm falling! You might not think so, but I am." We stopped at the end of the street. "Everybody wants me to listen to them, but no one will listen to me. They are my parents. I love them, Lea. Imagine if you hadn't seen your parents in six years? I need you to understand what this means to all of us. Grandma might never see us again —" The dam broke.

I'd never felt him shake before. "I'm here. I'm not going anywhere, Dima. I'll catch you." We embraced by the cherry blossom tree, my chin on his shoulder.

"Who cares if a piece of bread falls out of Grandma's mouth? Or if they take things from the fridge and 'mess it up'? Maybe you think they are overstepping their bounds — which I understand — but why can't you accept them doing that? I want them to be comfortable, to feel at home. They don't in any way mean to be rude."

"Do you think I make them feel uncomfortable?" I said.

"What makes them uncomfortable is our constant fighting," he said.

"It feels like you and your family are on one side of the battle ground, and I'm on another, in a different war. It feels like 'us' and 'you.' I know we're both feeling emotionally bruised, almost unable to control our actions and words. But our marriage is uncomfortable," I stopped. His family was blood, but it seemed they diluted the lines that drew us together. He stared into the sky.

"Does your family surprise you? Or do you remember the way it was in Russia and understand?"

"I can't say I'm used to it. I was surprised by some things. Completely forgot we didn't throw paper down the toilet, completely forgot that."

"What other things bothered you?" I asked.

"Well, if you think about it, everything bothers you. From the toilet, to rearing Viktor, to how I act. You can't deal with being told what to do, especially with the baby. Like, when they said that we should free his balls from the Pampers, I still think we should, or feed him homemade soup instead of jarred baby food — I mean, it's better to give the kid real food."

But I thought of how I had been told these things — instructed as though a child and not a mother and a wife. Be quiet. He needed me to listen and hold him. We both needed to let go of everything for a moment. It healed me to love him, and it seemed there was a way to make everything work. For now, it wouldn't be through figuring it out. It wouldn't be through mutual understanding. I still wasn't sure how, but I believed the only way was through faith and God's love. In Him we would stay together, changing for the better, learning to let go.

"We have to take Grandma to the hospital," he said, storming into our bedroom a couple days before the end. I set aside my book and glanced at the clock: 10:00 PM.

"What's wrong? Is she feeling worse?" I said.

"I called the doctor, told him her leg's purple in spots. He said she has an infection and needs to go the emergency room immediately." He moved to the hallway and I followed.

"What should I do?" I said.

"Just stay here and answer the phone. Mom and I are going to the hospital. I might be there all night —"

"What about work?"

"I'm going to the office tomorrow." It felt wrong, but I breathed a sigh of relief. We couldn't afford even an emergency of unpaid time off.

After they left, I sat at the kitchen table with my Bible and journal open next to a soggy bowl of cereal. Dima's father came into the kitchen for tea. I got the Russian-English dictionary from the bookshelf and tried to ask Viktor if Grandma had health insurance.

"I no understand," he said. I shook my head and repeated how difficult this was. We tried a few more times to understand each other and finally fell silent. I got up for tea. We had unearthed a packet of study materials Dima's host family had bought years ago, and Viktor went to his room to practice English.

The phone rang. "What's going on?" I asked Dima.

"Grandma has a severe infection from a fungus in her toenails. It's not healing because of diabetes. The doctors put I.V. drip in her arm and gave her morphine," he said.

"Is she going to be all right?" I asked. His father slumped in the kitchen chair, chin cradled in his hands.

"They can't say. The doctor's really nice, she's doing everything for Grandma — but the infection is really bad." Tatyana counted it a miracle to get a good doctor. She seemed to assume medical care in the States was as unpredictable as in Russia.

"How's Grandma?" I asked him.

"Totally out of it."

Dima never came home that night. I called Gotech Electronics the next morning on my way to teach at the University of Akron. "What's going on?" I asked him.

"The hospital just called. Grandma pulled her IV out. She won't let anyone come near her. They connected me to her room, and I heard her in the background repeating that she won't talk to anyone but her daughter or me. They tried to give her the phone, but she refused. 'Only in person,' she repeated in Russian. I have to go back to the hospital. I'm picking Mom up and going back."

"Does Jerry understand?" I asked.

"I think so, but what can I do?" I knew he was right; he had to leave Gotech. We would have to borrow money from my mother again.

At the hospital, Grandma was hysterical. "He's not Russian anymore! I'll only talk to Tatyana. She's still Russian! He's Americanized! He can't understand!" She shook her head adamantly.

"What drugs is she on?" Dima asked a doctor.

"We haven't been able to give her anything aside from the morphine last night and a bit of antibiotic through the IV before she tore it from her arm," the doctor said.

"The spies are in the outlet under the clock. I see them, Tonya. I know the nurses changed the time to confuse me. The clock's an hour ahead, I know!"

"Mom, it's okay. They are trying to help you —"

"Tonya! Everyone's talking about me and plotting to kill me! I want out of here right now," she kicked the sheet from her legs.

"Dima, we can't keep her here. We have to take her home. The morphine has her delusional. Please, ask the doctors what she can take orally. We must leave," his mother said.

Grandma returned to the small bed in the computer room, keeping her bottle of antibiotics on the windowsill behind her. Tatyana prepared her food, and Grandma trusted only her to serve it. Viktor was angry at her for upsetting us.

"Why did you buy more oatmeal and bread? We have a full loaf of the dark bread Grandma likes." I asked Dima.

"She won't eat that. She made us stop for new groceries before we came home. The medicine has her really whacked out."

"This is what communism does to a person," Viktor said, staring out the kitchen window.

"Can we pray?" I asked, feeling overcome with sadness.

"We need to find a prayer for Grandma's head," Viktor said. I would have prayed for that, but I supposed he meant this wasn't a prayer in his book.

"We've already been praying," Tatyana said, jiggling her leg under the table. "We are past prayer."

The night before they left early in September, Dima's body stretched out long and thin, the fan blowing on his backside. I lay next to him, turning off the light and cuddling against him. In the morning, we again packed the minivan, praying Grandma would make it home to her hospital without further complications. Dima drove the family to New York, walked them through JFK Airport, and waited until they boarded the twelve hour flight home.

I was beyond weary. Our home seemed an empty shell that first night without the family. I sensed Grandma in the computer room. "Are you all right, Babushka?" I whispered. Dima's sweatshirt was crumpled in the crib, bed sheets tangled. The internet was connected, the monitor showing where he had found the cheapest hotel rate between New York and Stow.

It was over.

It felt like someone had died.

Things were still spinning.

Tatyana was the mother of my son's father, and I loved her. In my mind, she strolled Viktor Jr. up and down our street in red and white clogs. She ladled our plates with onions and fish covered in a heavy blanket of shredded carrots. I cherished her passion — sharp sounds, steady hands, and her firm presence. I continued to see Viktor signing the cross over his round body, pasty legs jutting out of Dima's khaki shorts. He waved goodbye beside the rose bushes as I backed out of the driveway for the university that last morning. His heart was simple and full, and seemed to want to give us himself completely.

For a time, emotions were frozen, thawed with a touch, frozen again. I wondered how the tension, beyond words, would heal. Was unity possible with people who had lived such different lives? I believed in God's plan and tried to trust, but the feelings of sorrow were hard to endure. No amount of scrubbing could remove the changes left. And yet, even though Dima may not have believed it, I loved him somehow more, though it was often difficult to show it. Our marriage seemed shrouded with unspoken expectations. The weight of responsibility was more than words could bear. And so we kept quiet.

Dima found a hummingbird's nest shortly after Grandma and his parents left. He held the bits of powder blue shell in his palm. "Look. The beast next door got her." I followed him out the flimsy side door of our kitchen. Airy tufts of nest sprinkled the earth behind our gray bungalow in late afternoon. A deep breeze swept through my hair.

I looked at the gnarled cherry tree couched in our shallow backyard. "She'll just have to remake the nest."

## CHAPTER FOURTEEN

# Baptism

Simply
Going to the Church awakens hunger for it.
You want more.
Truly.
Peace.
Joy.
Otherworldliness.
Taste and see how good He is,
that's it.
All.
Guilt,
nothing but interference.
First or last,
come.
Be.
Taste and see how good He is.

We continued attending services at St. Nicholas. We learned the Liturgy and the appropriate times to make the sign of the cross. My parents stood beside us and we were a few pews behind the Georges' grown girls and their families. Though at times self-conscious, the experience of the Church was profoundly beautiful and peace could ease all earthly cares. I was joyful to simply be there. Peter and Sharon were in Uganda working as missionaries when Dima and I would be baptized with Viktor that December.

I sat on the lid of the toilet in my old robe and sifted through hair pins for the crosses Dima's parents had brought us. The Orthodox cross was nearly an inch long and the chain fell to the center of my chest. I felt eager and hesitant at once to wear it. I wanted to take the next step towards Christ and believed being baptized into the Orthodox Church was the way; however, I wished to take this step with full confidence. In my heart, there was conviction, but in my mind I still wondered how I, and those I'd known through the years, including family, could have missed the fullness of Christ. We'd sought the truth, loved God, striven to love each other; certainly there was a similar longing for God. I rejoiced that there was more to being Christian and that I might experience a fuller life in Christ, but I sorrowed with a perspective that some of what had seemed full was not. Still, He would brought us to the Church in the time and way that was His plan. Who was I to doubt? "I believe, help me in my unbelief," I prayed.

"You're not supposed to touch it until the baptism," Dima breathed. I pinched the cross rounded on all four angles. Beside Jesus' palms was the Russian abbreviation for Jesus Christ.

"How does it look?" He turned to the cat and stroked her shiny coat, tongue pushed against the inside of his lip.

"You shouldn't take it off once it's on," he said.

"Did you read that in the catechumen book your mother brought?" He nodded. I bowed my head, "What's it say here?" A prickly sensation crept up the backs of my arms with thoughts of the Russian priest who had blessed it. Our baptism was the coming together of East and West in Christ.

"Save and protect," he said, arching over me. I sounded out the letters, "Spasi i sokhrani."

After his parents left, I hung their gift of an icon of the Mother of God above the phone in our bedroom with dental floss. The Theotokos' face peered into mine when I played the answering machine messages. Walking through a late summer sunset with Viktor, my body eased into the cooling air and glided down the slight slope of road. The sun warmed my collarbone. I prayed with tears and swiped fingers under my sunglasses. "Mother of God," I whispered, "help me to never forget my calling as a mother. Help me to believe what is true." A breeze rustled through dark green branches.

"Momma?" Viktor twisted his little body in the stroller and stared up at me. Love ached for his cotton chest, small hands, and new hair.

Becoming Orthodox was a change in perspective and a developing understanding. I had never consciously eliminated mystery from Christianity. I would have admitted there was much that escaped explanation and reason in my faith at any time along the way. What I had begun to realize, though, was that the choice had been made by the tradition I followed, which had dismissed the saints, the Liturgy, the feasts and fasts, and the saving mystery of Holy Communion as the body and blood of Christ. If these elements were in the way of a relationship with Christ, why would they have ever been in practice by the Apostles? While things changed with time and place, Christ did not. Christians remained in Christ through seasons of fasting and feasting, sorrowing and rejoicing established by the Church. It was in the way of life that salvation history, the actual events, were remembered. However, in Liturgy and other services of the Church, by way of hymns, prayers, incense, prostrations — every act, mental and physical — the life of Christ was lived in the present. Protestants argued for a personal relationship with Jesus. In Orthodoxy, this was no less important. In addition, however, individuals realized their connectedness with others, particularly in Christ and His Church, but also beyond the Church. The faith became a way to care for all people in the love of Christ. It was this care that led people to the doors of Orthodox churches throughout the world. I thought of the beggar in Russia. The Church was a way of living that challenged selfishness. The choice to act in love was there, though one didn't always. The fullness of life in Christ was there, though some might have been in Orthodox churches for other reasons as superficial as culture. It hadn't ever been about the East or West but about Him whose love spanned the entire distance and beyond.

Many things about Orthodoxy colored a fuller picture of the faith I'd always had. According to the teachings of the Orthodox Church, the Incarnation of Christ, God becoming man, represented the purpose of art. "Art is, by definition, the use of material things as the medium for the revelation of God. So for the Orthodox, art is not icing on the cake; it is something very central to what we know of how God has revealed Himself to us."[1] Beauty and art were more than mere ornament, as had been argued since the ancients, and there was purpose and function as important as divine revelation. The world was full of many good things to revere. As Oscar Wilde wrote, "The true mystery of the world is the visible."[2]

In the Protestant tradition, the deliberate plainness of the church was arguably for attention to be on Christ. However, people were created sensate and it was harder to conceptualize Him and the kingdom of heaven without the icons, incense, candles, bells, and joyful sorrow in the hymnology of the Church. While I hadn't thought the plainness of Protestant churches revealed less of God, after attending Orthodox worship it was impossible to return without a sense of loss.

Back at church in Mentor, I walked to the front icon of the patron Saint Nicholas and uncomfortably bowed. It took time for an icon as a window through which I might glimpse the heavenly to feel like a spiritual experience. The saints saw me. They were alive in a dimension outside of time and place. While I chose to believe this based on the teachings of the ancient faith, these were new traditions that felt odd.

The next morning was overcast, and I hoped to get our walk in before the storm. I grabbed my cell phone and belted Viktor into the stroller under a threatening sky.

"Hi, Melanie. Are you changing the baby?" My niece cried. I pushed the stroller faster.

"Mary fell from the wall this morning," I said.

"What?" she laughed.

"You know the icon I hung in our bedroom? Well the floss broke, and I found her on the ground. I seriously wondered if maybe it was a sign. I mean, what if it is idolatrous?" Clouds gathered, and I hoped

---

[1] *The Orthodox Study Bible*, New King James Version, (Nashville: Thomas Nelson Publishers, 1993).

[2] "Strength to Love," http://poetryfoundation.org/bio/oscar-wilde 20 May 2011.

it wouldn't rain before we got home. Melanie and I had always shared our thoughts, but I did not want to confuse her about Orthodoxy. I did not want her to take my uncertainties too seriously, but I also didn't want to feel separated in any way from my sister. "I don't think so, though. I have sensed her, Melanie. Really. It's odd that we never thought about her before."

"Do you pray to her now?" she asked.

I told her I did, fully believing she offered help and protection. "The other evening when I was walking with Viktor, I felt her so strongly that I actually cried. Don't laugh," I chuckled with her. "I know this all sounds strange — but —" Help me Mother of God. "Words don't mean much without the experience. If the Georgeses had tried to explain Orthodoxy before I felt something was off at New Grace, I wouldn't have been interested."

"I know what you mean," she began. "You still like the praise and worship videos Aunt Vicki got the kids, right?" she asked.

"I like pop Christian music. I just don't see it as church music so much anymore." She said Aunt Vicki thought I was more excited about my church than God. She agreed and said Dad was too.

"But that's because it's so much more than just another church. It actually changes the way we see living our faith. It's not about a style of worship we prefer. In fact, personal preference is far from the point. As the undivided Church, the body of Christ, one continues experiencing new things — just related to ancient and universal other things. I mean, what if when we got to heaven we said we didn't like the style of God's uncreated light, that we preferred a softer glow, perhaps pinkish —" we giggled. The point was, we had to learn who God was, not who we wanted Him to be.

When the great composer Beethoven was asked what a song meant, he pondered the question and returned to his piano stool to play the piece again. Meaning was most fully realized in the experience. I read *Father Arseny: A Cloud of Witnesses*[3] later that night in

---
[3] p. 214.

bed. "All believers are members of the Church of Christ. Without the Church, it is difficult for one person alone to find the way of salvation, the right way to act in this earthly life. Outside the Church, a person ails." It was about being Christian. I thought of Peter Georges' recent email from Uganda: "Orthodoxy is a descriptive the Church Fathers used to differentiate the true faith from the heresies that were with the Church from the beginning." It wasn't about one church over another church, it was about being united as believers in Christ — this was and had always been the Church.

My parents and Dima and I were at St. Nicholas for an hour to learn about the Church before we were baptized. I had attended Bible studies during my days at Malone College and New Grace, but Fr. Andrew's approach was more formal. He cleared his throat and said we'd be using *The Anaphora of the Liturgy of St. Basil* as a study guide. Learning from a Liturgy contextualized with salvation history was a new concept for me, nothing like Rick Warren's devotional, *The Purpose Driven Life,* which we had studied in small groups at New Grace. The text had many allusions and references Father explained, and, unlike other Bible studies, we weren't to simply discuss our opinions on matters. The catechism was instructional of salvation history from the Old Testament. Anaphora meant lifting up and Liturgy meant common work. St. Basil was the fourth century bishop of Caesarea and one of the three holy hierarchs of the Church. Father said the greatest way to learn was to attend the services of the Church, paying attention to the feasts, fasts, and saints' days.

Trying to instruct others on a yearly cycle of faith best understood in a lifetime of experience must have been difficult for our priest. Though I saw he was uncomfortable, there was also a kind smile and determination to help us understand. He didn't seem to consider himself a source of wisdom and knowledge, which was different from university professors and many pastors I knew. There seemed a limitless well of history, tradition, and sacred practices, which Father introduced. I agreed with Dima, Orthodoxy would connect the dots for our family. Additionally, it related time and place throughout history and the world. Christianity had roots that connected each to a greater, more far reaching unity then one's individual life could.

Fr. Andrew was proud that there were ethnics as well as Americans worshipping together in his parish. His father was Russian, but he had grown up in America and believed the Church should be accessible to the time and place of all people, including Americans. He served in English. Head coverings were fine, but not necessary. I felt comfortable with Fr. Andrew. He had four children a few years younger than I. They were active in the parish and the world: an electrical engineer, a teacher, and two studying in college. His wife was also a teacher with a gift for children. The family embraced our baby joyously. Loud cries were merely "holy noise," they assured. Father had a drum set in his basement and wrote song lyrics. When preparing a non-fasting meal, he grilled burgers in khaki cutoffs. He spoke of love for his wife after twenty-five years of marriage. He was a normal American man and a true believer. It was natural to draw close to Father and his family; however, Orthodox Christianity was more than a lovely family. There was deeper spirituality possible, and it was this that made conversion most necessary.

After catechumen class, we sat at my parents' kitchen table finishing a meatloaf dinner. Mom seemed too quiet and serious. "I've got to finish some work at Gotech," Dima said. Instead of arguing that he was working too hard and could spend time with my family (the way I had with his) I waved goodbye. I wanted to be alone with Mom and Dad and continue discussing Orthodoxy.

My mother bustled the dishes to the sink and interrupted my father and me. "Are you going to eat your cookie?" she asked.

"Who cares about the cookie?"

"Who cares about church!" she said. I stormed upstairs to brush my teeth and stifle my tears. I hated that she wouldn't just come around, just think about it. It was finally the church where we could stay.

"Lea. Are you upset?" she asked and settled on the landing outside the bathroom. The toothbrush stuck out of my sudsy mouth.

Spitting and mumbling "I'm fine," I wiped my mouth on the Christmas towel that smelled of cinnamon candles. Dad walked upstairs into his room, rattling in his change cup for the ChapStick. My parents and I settled into the hallway just as we had so many times growing up. Little Viktor crawled over my mother's pink sweatpants.

My mother began, "I agree with the stance of the Orthodox Church. I really do. It's —"

"Diane, it's undivided. You aren't going to get a church more the way Christ intended outside of Orthodoxy. Trust me," my father said.

"I agree. I just — I feel judged."

"From who?" Dad asked.

"From Father, from people at church, everyone."

"Mom, I know how you feel. I've felt that way, too. It's like you have to explain you're a Christian even though you're not Orthodox."

"Yeah, and I don't like that. I don't like the exclusivity of the church. It feels cold and too foreign. I hate the bells, and it's so hot in there. I just don't like it, and I don't know why I'm the only one who feels this way." My father stared at a patch of carpet.

He said, "But the Church doesn't judge those outside of Orthodoxy. We don't know anyone's heart but our own. We're not supposed to determine who's 'saved.' In fact, that's part of what bothers me about the Protestant tradition. We've been going to all these protesting congregations searching for the undivided Church for years!"

"So, are you telling me that there won't be differences among Orthodox churches?" Mom said.

"I don't know why you're fighting so hard against all of this. You're usually the most saintly of us all. But you're so stubborn on this one." I smiled at my father's words. Mom was the first to pass up dinner to watch Viktor so I could eat, the first to apologize and insist on hugs and kisses before anyone left, the first to smile and ask how we were, listening and rarely complaining. My mother wanted peace among the family, and dividing from my sister and Aunt Vicki challenged acceptance of new church traditions. She didn't want to consider faith as it had been practiced in the past because it didn't seem to matter for her life today. Even though she too was discontent with Protestantism, she didn't want to change. I didn't have the years, doubt, or same depth of divide that kept my mother hesitant. I expected understanding from my mother that she wasn't able to have just then.

I fell into the couch downstairs, Dima asleep upstairs. Maybe his family would connect through Orthodoxy, but mine was dividing. Thoughts rolled cold under my skin as I opened my prayer book. "I pray, O Virgin: dispel the storm of my sorrows and spiritual turmoil. You are the bride of God who bore the origin of stillness and alone are most pure." I liked not needing new words for age-old feelings. I longed to perceive my life as one piece to a larger whole.

After Divine Liturgy the next morning, I sought Father. We talked in the corner of the banquet hall as people buzzed with coffee and bagels. I sat next to him a table away from my mother feeding Viktor peaches. I was certain my faith was as it had always been — regardless of the church I attended—about my relationship with Jesus Christ. I wanted to tell Father this. I needed to know that he understood Protestants were also Christians.

"The Orthodox tradition uses rituals as tools that draw one into the Christian experience. If you can understand the language, the mood, and the atmosphere, then you are drawn into it and the mystery comes. It's not a science," he smiled. "It's all about the unchanging nature of Jesus Christ."

"Maybe we realize His unchanging nature when we are willing to change," I said.

At Christmastime, my first confession just before our baptisms, I took my journal and weathered NIV Student Bible, stuffed with scraps of scribbled on bulletins from New Grace. Only those newly entering the Church were confessing. There were a few couples besides us. The sanctuary was dark, cold, and silent. A deacon illumined the icons with votive candles, and a woman chanted the gospel at the front of the sanctuary, opposite to where the confessor and priest would be. Despite the soft colors and chanting, deep chills settled inside that had little to do with the cool sanctuary.

Why did I need to confess my sins to Father? Couldn't I just talk things over with God on my own? People said we'd feel so much better. I didn't ask how so, or why, or what if I didn't really have all that many big sins to confess. I went hoping for a deeper peace and understanding. I approached Father and faced the icon of Christ above the golden Bible placed on a podium at my shoulders. I didn't know where to direct my eyes and stared straight ahead. Was I talking to God? To Father?

"I confess that I put my routine before my family."

"What do you mean 'routine,'" Father asked.

"Like my morning jog and writing. I can't seem to settle or appreciate Dima and my Mom when they interrupt my routine."

"It's not bad to be disciplined," Fr. Andrew began. But I wanted to start over and say I was frantic, consumed, constantly pushing, impatient, furious with nervous energy. I was afraid.

I left more confused than comforted. Change wouldn't be easy, or it would be more of the same. Sometimes I wished things could stay the same. Or that I could maintain unwavering faith despite change — in God, in the truth that I hoped He was revealing through the people and situations we faced. I was unsure how to stay close with family who suddenly had a different perspective. I was too excited to calmly accept that each was on a faith journey. It was never the way of the Church to push faith onto another. We were to love and accept our family, our friends, even our enemies.

The bottom line was simple and clear. The truth of the Church was not a choice, though I had a choice to be a part of it. It was the undivided Church. Apostolic tradition. The Church in heaven.

How do I know Lord?

You believe.

I set two alarms the December morning of our baptism. They both went off despite warnings that Satan might complicate things. Little Viktor was hysterical — bottom as red as a chimpanzee's. "Great. Dima? Please help me over here. I can't do this without you!" I grew frantic as Viktor's wailing climaxed. I cupped a poopy diaper in one hand, in the other, his squirming legs held at the ankles like a raw chicken. A groggy Dima emerged from the corner.

"Oh great. His butt is raw. This is ridiculous. What are we going to do? I told you we should have let him sleep without the diaper. My mom was right. The plastic diapers are terrible for him. Think about it," he said.

"No, you not changing him yesterday and his sitting in crap made this worse!" Viktor's little arms flailed and he twisted onto his stomach. "Just grab the cream on the dresser. We've only got twenty minutes. Come on, we have to go," I said. After a whirlwind of bags, bottles, purse, and cameras, we were in the Camry for the stretch to St. Nicholas. Sun fell on the salt streaked windshield. I closed my eyes, and Dima put his hand on my thigh.

"It's okay. We'll get to church on time. Everything's fine." I was determined to be silent until my words were civil. We had agreed to give ourselves plenty of time, to actually not race out of the house. To be ready for our baptisms — spirits, minds, bodies. But as usual, we had left with clothes strewn over the couch, Viktor's uneaten oatmeal on a plate without Saran Wrap, and knots drawn tight inside. My shoulders eased, head rolled — Viktor shrieked. "Okay. It's okay." Dima mumbled as much to himself as to Viktor and me. "I'm going to turn Neal Young on. It'll help, trust me." Neal Young's steady guitar silenced our son every time.

We pulled into the parking lot at nine-thirty. "How do you feel, Dima?"

"I'm good. This feels right."

"It really does."

The foyer was packed with our family, much to my surprise. I hadn't extended official invitations, figuring our family would rather not directly endure the strangeness. I approached Susan, wrapping my arms around her black mink.

"I'm glad you could make it with the holiday open-house today and everything," I said and turned to hug Jerry, grazing his cheek with a kiss.

"We wouldn't miss Viktor's baptism," she said. I hung our coats, Dima stuffing Viktor's into the sleeve of his. My face was hot. Aunt Vicki stood against the cool window next to my sister's family.

"Hey, guys! I'm so happy you're here." Aunt Vicki's velvet scarf smelled of powdery musk. Prayers stilled my nerves and I was in the moment.

Father roamed his short fingers over Viktor in the sign of a cross. I stared at a patch of red carpet. Father breathed gently in my face, signed the cross over me, and laid his right hand on my head. "I lay my hand upon Your servant, Lea, who has been found worthy to flee unto Your holy name, and to take refuge under the shelter of Your wings." I breathed deeply as he continued praying over Viktor. "Be gone, and depart from this sealed, newly enlisted warrior of Christ our God. For I charge you by Him who rides upon the wings of the wind, and makes His angels spirits, and his ministers a flaming fire: be gone, and depart from this created one, with all your powers and your angels." Father breathed blessings in the form of a cross over our mouths, brows and breasts. Our voices were a tight chord. Chills raced up my arms.

"Do you unite yourself to Christ?"

"We do unite ourselves to Christ."

"Have you united yourselves to Christ?"

"We have united ourselves to Christ."

"Do you believe in Him?"

"We believe in Him as King and God."

After the baptism, Viktor and I stood before the bathroom mirror, our crosses gleaming. Holy water dripped onto the shoulders of my robe, rolled down my neck. Sweet oil glistened above my lips — Lord Jesus, be upon me forever. I wanted to always see the commitment I had made to the Lord. I wanted to feel the heavenly peace and joy alive in those moments. I hadn't felt so beautiful since the day Dima and I had married.

Viktor's hands shook as he grabbed Cheerios from a wrinkled baggie. He giggled as I kissed his forehead, inhaling his soft skin. My eyes were moist as a woman from the parish entered. "Do you need some help, honey?"

"That would be great. I just want to run out and get my purse. I think I left it with my coat."

Susan and Jerry were slipping out of Liturgy. "We have to go. There are still things we need to do for the party," Mrs. Holmes said.

"I'm glad you could come," I said.

The rest of the family spilled from the sanctuary. "We just want to leave before Communion," my mother said with a meek smile. Dad's face was blank. Aunt Vicki didn't meet my eyes. After Liturgy, parishioners hugged and kissed us; they stuffed cards and icons in my purse. The Georges' girls ordered cake and pizza for the coffee hour in our honor. Hope and love were palpable among those at St. Nicholas on that morning. I longed to share life with them, in all its seasons.

On the way to Susan's open-house, Dima and I talked about Christianity in Russia. In the Soviet Union, "Christmas" had been Winter Solstice celebrated on the seventh of January. Stashed in one of our Russia photo albums was a snapshot of Dima clad in party hat and old fashioned bloomers suspended halfway up his belly. Grandpa Frost and the Snow Queen sat by his side. "Is Grandpa Frost like St. Nicholas?" I asked.

"He loved children and spread goodwill, so yeah. Nothing could change the people's traditions. The communists just changed names and destroyed churches. They couldn't take Christianity out of the country, no matter how hard they tried."

"How did your family celebrate Christmas back home?" I asked.

"We didn't, really."

The Holmes' open-house was thick with wine and oil, perfume and laughter. Picking at a plateful of small egg rolls and shrimp cocktail, I told Susan, "I didn't know so much of the family would want to come to the baptisms. I didn't think my family was interested in the Orthodox Church." She continued arranging appetizers and responded that it was just a church.

Mr. Holmes waived his hand over his head, smiling as two guests followed him to the living room. "Tea, anyone?" He served green tea in tiny wooden cups. He called me into the foyer. "I bought this in Russia," he nodded to a bronze icon of Christ hanging eye level next to the grandfather clock.

"That's beautiful." I looked down at the silver cross around my neck. Joy continued there with our family, and life seemed inexhaustibly wonderful.

Dima and I shuffled Viktor to bed and settled together in the kitchen. He grabbed the cordless to call his parents while I unwrapped our new icons. Russian. I smiled with the familiar sounds. The jangle of the language moved through the kitchen.

My mind flashed back to hours ago when Viktor had been in the arms of Father. He had offered our son to Dima who carried him around the sacred altar. Afterwards, I had gathered him from the step at the front of the church as a gift from God. His small fingers had pressed my shoulders. Joy filled me in a very quiet way.

"What did your parents have to say?"

"Mom said she's glad we've reached this conclusion. Come here." I stepped into his embrace, still and warm, faith as real as the man who held me. Faith — in God, in family — was mystery. And I was hopeful, the ineffaceable touch of God like a feather on my skin.

# IV

## SETTLING INTO FAITH AND FAMILY

"The Lord will command His loving kindness in the daytime, and in the night His song shall be with me — a prayer to the God of my life."*

"Each must find his or her own way and glorify God through it. Ultimately, this is all that matters. The rest is detail."**

---

\* *The Student Bible*, New International Version, (Grand Rapids: Zondervan Publishing House, 1996), Psalm 42.8.

\*\* Protopresbyter Thomas Hopko, St. Nicholas Orthodox Church Church Bulletin, Mentor, OH, 2008.

**CHAPTER FIFTEEN**

# Baby Blues

New babies, like new faith, like a new homeland, are often accompanied by inconsolable tears. After the summer visit, we had less than two years before his parents would move to America. We were blessed with another son, Dominik, and developed friendships with our church family at St. Nicholas. Dima's parents were preparing to leave Russia, more willing than ever now that Grandma had fallen asleep in the Lord, just a few months after returning from America. Russia seemed increasingly corrupt, and though they mourned separation from lifetime friends, they longed to become more familiar with us.

I glanced at the clock on the small table between the bed and the rocking chair: 6:45 AM It was Saturday on Labor Day weekend, but every day felt drowned in the monotony of motherhood. The baby would need nursed soon. I rolled onto my back to say my morning rule of prayer, at least the parts I could recall without the Orthodox prayer book, but felt completely unmoved. I sighed, asked the Lord to help me pray, and made the sign of the cross, turning to cross Dima whose hot leg was too close to mine. His eyes peeped open groggily, my right hand mid-air. I smiled at him.

"Read your essay about me," he mumbled. My smile melted. I had written countless essays about him that expressed my love. Recently, however, I had needed to write through why I had been tucked away in bed, or with a child, or on the computer — too busy for him, beyond necessity. I wondered what it meant to lose the magic of romance, the thrill of love, the energy of marriage, easier in the beginning, only seven years ago.

I began to downplay my doubts and then let go of controlling the situation. "It's how I felt," I said. There was nothing to explain. It didn't seem circumstances that tested my emotions, though having money and time to share with him might have seemed a balm. Love was layered. It seemed the deeper we tread through the stratum of our life, the more feelings transitioned. Along with the strain, Dima and I shared the smooth cheek of our newborn, the giggles of our toddler, the afternoon breeze floating through our kitchen with a hint of garlic. Faith was loving him.

The air was crisp. Trees darkened with the end of summer. The American flag flapped against our home, honoring Labor Day and the war in Iraq, five years and still rolling on. Dima and Viktor Jr. were fishing on Lake Erie in my father's small aluminum boat. I sat cross-legged on the carpet in the living room beside our four month-old intently slobbering over his fists, kicking tiny toes in the air. I began reading an account of the Orthodox saint, Mother Mary of Egypt.

As the story went, a monk had lived at a monastery since childhood and thought he'd attained spiritual perfection. He went on a pilgrimage into the desert and discovered a woman, naked and dark with white, wool-like hair. The vision brought him unspeakable joy. He knew she would illumine truth that would somehow strengthen his faith in God.

After the monk introduced himself, the woman shared the story of her life with him. She said she had wandered the desert for forty-seven years after living in Egypt as a prostitute. When she had been in the world, she had satisfied great lusts for wine and men, food and every pleasure that consumed the flesh. One day, she saw a group of Egyptians hurrying to the sea for a journey to Jerusalem for the Elevation of the Honorable Cross. She followed, hoping to sleep with young men on the pilgrimage, and was successful in her pursuit. She followed the people to church once the hour came for the Elevation of the Cross, but a power kept her from entering the sanctuary. At once, she realized her sin. She tried to enter four times before praying to the Mother of God to allow her to repent and enter. Once inside the church, she vowed to live her life completely in honor of God. In that very moment, she chose to believe, her faith became full of life.

While in the desert, she longed for the pleasures of the world. Without food or clothing, shelter or companionship, she survived on things found among the sand and barrenness. Faith burned within her and so did doubt and temptations to return to the world. The woman continued on and fed on incorruptible food and the hope of salvation, as she told the monk. When the monk asked how she knew the Psalms, as she had no Bible and had never been taught from it, she said that the Word of God, living and active, itself teaches knowledge to man (Heb. 4:12). Love was faith in action.

Her humility allowed belief in God; she chose to love Him more than herself. She gave her life reciprocating love unto God. As the story went, she lifted in the air when she prayed in tongues the monk could not understand. She walked across the Jordan. She prophesied. The monk had not obtained such spiritual gifts. Through Mary, formerly a prostitute, the monk, who thought he had reached spiritual perfection, learned the cost of choosing faith and acting in love.

My body was stiff as I stood from the floor and drifted into the kitchen for a plate of ginger cookies and a glass of milk. My mouth watered, though I'd eaten a thick sandwich minutes earlier. I couldn't imagine: no tasty treats, no hot shower, no sex — no distractions to the attention of my soul, that inner voice that craved something beyond me, something more silent than silence, more warm and comforting than wine. I wondered, though, in the world, what was faith? What did it look like?

My mother and I had walked around Silver Lake on an overcast afternoon a few days earlier. We had talked of marriage, how the magical feelings fade. Geese squawked as my laughing toddler closed in on them. It seemed love for each other, like faith in God, was a choice. At first, the choice was soft, the other person eliciting excitement within one's self. At first, the pressure was light, everything new and possible. But life branched out, stretching beyond one's self, and became weightier.

Walking back home in a drizzle, my mother mentioned hearing on the radio how Mother Teresa doubted God throughout her life. The saint had written letters to her church spiritual guides in the 1950's and 1960's that were forgotten until two years ago when the Vatican had gathered paperwork on Mother Teresa for sainthood. In one letter she wrote, "Love — the word—it brings nothing. In my soul, I can't tell you how dark it is, how painful, how terrible — I feel like refusing God."[1]

As we walked on, the colorless day seeped into me, everything seeming dull and monotonous. Mother Teresa had lived in the world. She had known the pains of recent times and somehow chosen faith, even when she felt empty. She acted on her faith in God — serving the poor and needy through her old age. She loved people as the way to loving God.

I stared out the window as the baby cooed and reached for his toes. Dima and I had been married on a brilliant summer day. We had held each other and slowly moved to Al Green's *Let's Stay Together*. It had been easy to feel love, to choose to stay together. Faith had spread as naturally as the setting sun, love burning as radiant. Maybe it was also this way with our love for God — easy in the beginning, and harder as life cost us more and more. The flag billowed with the summer breeze. I wondered if Dima and I could find the energy and interest in a slow dinner talking patiently with one another, beyond the everyday worries of life. Perhaps feelings encouraged one to choose faith in God, in each other, but these faded in time. Enduring faith was acting in love even when the feelings were as flat, or, as with Mother Teresa, the soul's darkness was so painful that we felt like denying God. Always, there was the humbling choice to weather the season that no longer made me feel good and hope the young, green leaves would come

---

[1] Brian Kolodiejchuk, M.C. ed., *Mother Teresa Come Be My Light: The Private Writings of the "Saint of Calcutta,"* (New York: Doubleday, 2007).

again. Or, with fear so easily clouding faith in love, with doubt always so near, I could deny hope. I could fail to love.

My parents were chrismated into the Faith our first Pascha. That first Easter in the Church, my mother's reading glasses perched on the tip of her nose, hand on her back. After leading the procession around the church, my parents and Dima and I had slipped into the crowd of faithful close to Father at the front. Everything was bright: vestments, lights, hymns. Everything that happened seemed to be about me but not within me. I was among the Church, the angels in heaven, all the heavenly hosts, but I felt what my mother expressed beside me. It was unending, confounding, dramatic — and all of it made me conscious of the ignorance from which I came. After the Paschal Service, it was almost one in the morning when a rustle spread through the faithful and the Divine Liturgy began. During Sundays, it had been difficult to endure the length and added Lenten hymns, but this first Pascha seemed endless.

Around three in the morning, we gathered for the blessing of the baskets of cheese and Pascha breads, wine, flavored vodkas, chocolates, and other morsels of non-Lenten delicacies. My parents had packed fried chicken and beer. We laughed, feeling mildly nauseous; next year we'd make bread, choose wine, perhaps a Russian sausage. I was outside the banquet, peering in by the drinking fountain when Fr. Andrew caught my eye after blessing the baskets. He smiled and light radiated from his eyes and skin. He was aglow. In that instant, I wanted what was within him. Seeing joy incarnate in a man who had not tried to convince me of anything, who answered simply and to the point, his clear teaching and honest heart present in each note he offered, seeing Fr. Andrew that first Pascha was more convicting than anything I had ever experienced. I would need this image of pure joy and light, for becoming Orthodox was about to cost me.

At St. Nicholas, my mother felt hot, wearied, and overwhelmed by the strong scent of incense, the hard to follow Liturgy, and the intensity of time and attention that was the way in the Orthodox tradition. While there were degrees of engagement with the Orthodox way of life, just as there were in the Protestant traditions, my mother and father wanted to be active and embrace the life of the Church in which they served. Just stay, wait, be. My parents wanted to fit into the fullness of Orthodoxy sooner than seemed possible. They had been Christians most of their lives, without the sacraments and holy Tradition, and was difficult to understand the necessity in changed perspective. My sister wasn't there, nor were the many friends and family members, alive and passed on, with whom we shared this life. The gap between their past and present experiences in Christianity was insurmountable for my parents at this time. It killed the clear need to change.

When I considered how my parents were always seeking God, I began to see how the American way of life conditioned expectations for rational, individualistic approaches to Him. Church was before a day with the family on the lake. Church services were an hour, easy to understand, and efficient. If not, there was no reason to stay. The drawing together of different languages and people in all times and places in the life of Christ was a mystery difficult to conceive from a Protestant perspective. It was a phenomenon one might accept in concept but when experienced it included elements of worship that were foreign to Protestant traditions. Furthermore, the very essence of Protestantism, protesting tradition and sacraments that seemed unnecessary, fueled a resistance difficult to penetrate. The only way would be to accept what couldn't be readily understood and to endure the oddity of a tradition not yet one's own, but with faith that it was the way to God. My parents experience in the Church was different from mine and less satisfying. After a year, they left the Orthodox Church.

The way of life offered through Orthodoxy helped me understand the dynamics of my family and realize the need to unite in Christ. The Orthodox Faith allowed attention to a need deep inside me, which hadn't found expression in the Christian life I had known before, but this wasn't the experience just yet for my parents. I believed, however, that we would be together at the chalice in time.

When Dima's parents came to live in America, no one supported them as they seemed to expect. While our family gave things, spent time, hosted dinners, hope ebbed. Quiet between Dima and me began to deepen with our family divided by unexplained anger and hurt. Perhaps he feared I couldn't handle the cost of his parents in our lives, and perhaps I couldn't, had it not been for a way of life in Christ that continually reminded me to love — as Christ loved me. Still, acting in love in real-life situations was trying.

For the first months, Tatyana and Viktor lived in our home. They had money from having sold their apartment and Grandma's and planned to buy a house as soon as possible. It would only be a matter of months. It was dark and breezy on Halloween night. Viktor Jr. was not yet three, and, despite my mother's, "it's fun for the kids," we'd opted to turn off the lights and hideout in the family room. Every day for the past week since the parents had come had felt like trick-or-treat, and we were exhausted.

Earlier in the week, I'd noticed a day in honor of Saint Dimitri on the Orthodox Church calendar. Though we had been Orthodox two years, the feasts and fasts remained mostly unfamiliar. With small inquiries, I moved deeper into the traditions and culture of the Church, often probing when something suddenly became of interest, like my husband's name and patron saint day.

Saint Dimitri was a third century saint in Thessalonica. He was commander of an army and had wealth and respect from men and even the Emperor. But when he was ordered to slaughter Christians in Thessalonica and he refused, his good life crumbled. He was imprisoned and executed. Faith had cost him everything.

As morbid as it sounded, dying for my faith could seem easier than living it. Lately, busyness left me desperate for pause, even withdrawal, from accomplishing life. Nursing our six month-old in the quiet nook of our bungalow excused me from the race. Instead of finding oil for Dima's father to fix the squeaking bathroom door; instead of convincing Tatyana that Dominik was too young for dark breads and thick cereals; instead of forcing socks on Viktor's freezing feet, bribing him into his underwear — I sat still and prayed: "Lord Jesus Christ, have mercy on me, a sinner." Sometimes it seemed impossible to resurface from the tidal wave of needs. Sometimes prayer was only stale words and another link in routine.

Somewhere along the course of these recent days, what it meant to feel happy changed — it always had been changing — as calm began to seem the center of true joy. I remember as a child praying for perfection. Mind, body, and spirit all working well and toward the goals I'd set: "Jesus help me ace this test; Jesus help me win the hundred-meter dash; Jesus help me be liked at school." Happiness had always seemed fast-moving, quick-effecting, self-appeasing — childish.

Still only possible with a childlike spirit, natural to the human condition and seemingly essential to faith in God, accepting the grace of faith was the only way to calm. Joy — deep, merciful, unrelenting — was independent of life's circumstances. Joy — enduring, steadfast, regenerative — was Love.

A night before Divine Liturgy, I was tangled in a web of anxiety. Viktor was coughing; I set up the humidifier. Dominik was teething; I dragged myself to him and nursed every three hours. Dima was sleeping; I pulled the quilt tighter around me, willing anxiety to relent. When sleep finally came, I was on a sinking ship. Warm water, pale light — an otherworldly carelessness seeped through me. My body became dizzy without air, pressed of life, finally expressed of earthly cares. Energy slipped through me, and I did not fear death; I longed for sweet release. I have heard that it is easier to endure death without thinking about it than to endure the thought of death without dying, and for the first time I felt the truth of this as I woke to the baby crying, to night fading, to day calling.

The next morning, I lumbered into the Povozhaev Express behind Dima's parents and our boys' car seats. My stomach ached, eyes felt dry and heavy, and car sick rolled through me as we rumbled down the highway to church. It was easy to feel sorry for myself and not to notice blessings. I read how the world could feel cool and seemingly without the love of Christ, but He remained in all and through all. I appreciated the depth of the Orthodox Faith. The obvious unrest of life was observed, and yet there was also hope. Christ would make all that had turned in on itself, all that had ceased glorifying him, beautiful once again. It was a miracle that in each Divine Liturgy, God was present on earth. During each Liturgy, Christ conquered the devil and death. He was here in each life situation, no matter what I felt or failed to feel, and though His promise to save us would be complete in the future, there was goodness now as well. Still, my body was heavy, and the day seemed too long to endure.

The family approached the doors of the church: Viktor running ahead in Spiderman shoes from Deydushka, the infant brightly hatted in the carrier under Babushka's arm, Dima sandwiched between me and his father. Freeing a hand from diaper bag, purse, baby, I gripped a beeswax candle and entered the sanctuary. The church was warm with incense and familiar faces, and it was as though I could feel prayers rising around me. I moved to the front of the church, kissed the icon of St. Nicholas, stood before the Theotokos and offered a quick prayer for our family, placing the candle beside others.

It was not long before the baby was fussing, and I was outside the sanctuary, outside the rich atmosphere of peace I longed for. I resented my situation: balancing the baby on the table by the door, pushing up my bra, wrestling the baby blanket over shoulder, breast, baby. A woman passed through the doors from the sanctuary and asked how I was. I mumbled that I have been better and returned to the sanctuary with the baby, jiggling him on my hip in the back of the church where we waited for Holy Communion.

"Receive the Body of Christ. Taste the Fountain of Immortality," we sang and slowly walked towards the chalice. I approached Father with the baby in my arms, turning him to receive the Body and Blood of Christ. "The child of God, Dominik, partakes of the most precious and holy Body and Blood of our Lord and God and Savior Jesus Christ for the remission of sins and life eternal." It was so clear in my soul — only one thing needful. "The handmaiden of God, Lea, partakes of the precious and most holy Body and Blood of our Lord and God and Savior Jesus Christ for the remission of sins and life eternal." I closed my eyes as the small gold spoon left my mouth, the mystery so warm and good.

Later, I wondered, how had I ever been better than when Christ was among us? So obviously, I took the joy of my salvation for granted — all that it meant to be a Christian stripped down to a matter of my own whimsical emotions. Still, no matter what I felt, God was God, and returning to peace and love was possible.

When Dima's parents had come to America two summers earlier, there had seemed a very different spirit of silence between us. Perhaps because the situation was temporary, and we'd had expectations that were unrealistic. Everything began on a different playground this time. In the corner of their bedroom, the parents' gold icons of Christ and the Theotokos were the same as those they'd given us last visit. Alongside these was a very old icon of the Family Protectors. A priest in Russia had blessed each of the icons, and though the parents had opened a window and crisp air slipped in, the room felt warm. It was in a spirit of hope that we all operated now: hoping to become family, hoping to become knowable to each other, hoping to share faith—in each other, in God. I began to sense that hope followed the decision to love, and that where there was hope and love, faith took root.

The process: deciding to love, accepting hope despite my doubt, and nurturing faith with a humble heart—this was the Christian way of life. A way of life I'd never attain. Once, I had prayed and believed God would relieve me of a given challenge, that His love saved me from hell, hell as torture and pain; hell as earthly experience, without His mercy. I hadn't thought (as Saint Silouan suggested[2]) "to hold my mind in hell, and not to despair" as the way to humility, and as the way towards His will for me. I hadn't considered that as the soul moved towards God it would, indeed that it should, become fearful, as Saint Silouan said:

---

[2] "On Humility," 13 Nov. 2007, www.orthodoxphotos.com.

> [B]ut when it sees the Lord, then it becomes immensely joyous from the beauty of His glory, and it forgets everything earthly in the face of the love of God and the sweetness of the Holy Spirit. This is the Lord's Heaven. Love will surround everyone, and from the humility of Christ they will be glad to see others above them.

Anxiety and darkness revisited the heart, the mind, just as they retreated. Too little attention was given to the process of life — in fact, the process as the way of life, the way towards eternal life.

Whatever the challenge: family, career, health, the test was to sustain, to find anew, hope. It seemed if I could love Dima, his parents, my children, then the protective shield of faith would serve to buffer the sure blows of discouragement and fatigue, of doubt and egotism. What did it mean to be humble, to be glad to see others above me? I thought it impossible to accept with a glad heart the loud silence of dinner: Russian conversation bouncing around the mix-matched plates, a baby grabbing my hair, salad falling from my fork. Selfishness was always so quick to challenge peace and push away calm.

This was the natural human way of things. Despite faith in God, the often silent undercurrent remained the belief that one should not be wronged. Not by man, not by God. It was hard to understand that comfort was not always God's way. In faith I accepted that suffering was somehow integral to life, but accepting and even enduring was not enough. To be joyful was necessary and could seem difficult.

This Halloween night, Dima had taken the parents to Wal-Mart to develop pictures from their last days in Russia. I cuddled on the floor with Viktor. We held dinners of hot cereal, and I giggled against his soft cheek. *The Snow Queen*, an animated European tale, played from the DVD. The Snow Queen's words were hollow sounding: "There is no love, no hope, no joy. There are no flowers, only icicles, Kay."

But the boy insisted, "There are roses, and they smell sweet, and there is love!"

"Sometimes, the cold is too much for mortals," the Snow Queen breathed. My son was frightened and cuddled closer against me, his toes freezing. My hands were warm from the mug of hot cereal, and I warmed him. I was often cold, and Dima warmed me, thick blood rarely leaving his hands cool. It seemed when I needed something for someone else, warmth for my boy, I had enough to give, and in the process was warmed myself.

All too often, the cold kept me uncomfortable and self-focused. All too often, faith in my thoughts and feelings weakened faith in God, love for family. Earlier that day, I'd called my mother frantically snapping Viktor into the stroller and throwing the Snugli (kangaroo-like infant carrier) in the base of the stroller. "I don't know where the parents have taken my baby! I can't stand this. Dima and I are going to need counseling — he would sacrifice our boys to save his parents from hurt feelings. They don't speak English. What if something happened — I don't trust any of this."

As I fumed, I found Dominik. They had been on a walk down the street for bread and milk. They had the baby bundled and smiling in the old pram. My mother's calm words played in my mind: "Think how they feel. Where are they to go; what are they to do?" It was undeniable, my life was once again in their hands, and I couldn't entirely shake the trauma. Two years ago, when the parents had left under a cloud of doubt, faith in God had been shaded as we struggled to maintain ourselves. In the course of the days until now, faith had permanently changed. It became more realized: the lack of faith, the need for faith. This was to be our life, and we had to try to come together in love.

I suddenly noticed there were no children at our door. I guessed Halloween trick-or-treating had been scheduled for a different day. I swallowed the warm cereal in my mug and thought to fold the endless piles of laundry in the utility room. Viktor hugged my neck too hard, more an act of little boy aggression than love, and I snapped. He reacted, said, "I no like you," and reminded me again how slippery human emotion was.

Contrary to our human reason, and as Fr. John Breck[3] suggested, "genuine faith is grounded in certainty that His absence is merely our perception of things, our short-sightedness, our stiff-necked blindness. What makes people truly holy is not a perpetual inner state of joy, peace, hope and faith. It is caring for the needy when they themselves feel spiritually abandoned." I had always been willing to embark upon ambitious projects — I'd be a missionary, I have said. How ludicrous, I suddenly realized, when my family was my mission. It was easier to imagine a faraway land of opportunity, more for myself than for others, as the special place God had for me. Folding my in-laws laundry, hunting for matches to socks, this wasn't my calling. At least it didn't feel so.

Later that night, Dima's father held a recent photograph of his eighty-year-old mother, a brother and cousin, the rest of his family still living in Siberia. They sat shoulder to shoulder around an old table with glass plates and flowered china bowls: cheese and sour cream potatoes, sardines, grape leaves stuffed with beef and rice, tomatoes and cucumbers. Behind his mother was an icon corner. The language wasn't there to ask what he thought about our becoming family; what he believed about God; how he wanted to live in America. When would we agree that pork roast might wait for a non-fasting day and skip the tea on Sunday morning? When would we hold steady with each other's eyes, neither feeling impatient or insecure with what was between us? Could we see the one thing needful? If only we gave attention to it, it would direct all our words and actions toward love.

On this Halloween night, the cold air whipped the frail birch tree outside, but Dominik was warm against my skin in the semi-dark of the baby's nook. The parents had never celebrated with Jack-o-Lanterns, had never roamed door-to-door for trick-or-treat. A people didn't need a tradition to recognize spirits of darkness about us. Within, doubts and fears tricked and treated us at their whim. I

---

[3] "Journey Through the Darkness," *St. Nicholas Orthodox Church Bulletin*, 4 Nov. 2007.

rocked the baby, Dima, his parents, the world: "Lord Jesus Christ, have mercy on me, a sinner."

Dima's parents settled into their own home around the corner from us. They hosted dinners and we came. Dima spent too many nights eating at his mother's table without me and the boys, but he patiently listened to my concern and we went together more often. Tatyana watched the boys, but this faded as she and Dima's father became busy with their own work, his mother cleaning and caring for an elderly Russian woman and his father working in the warehouse at Mr. Holmes' company with Dima. There was a lack of familiarity among us. While the children warmed up to play, laughing themselves to tears as Dyedushka lurched after them under a crocheted blanket playing monster, they didn't share the time or communication that they did with other family. There was the language barrier and Tatyana's inability to drive, which kept the children housebound and watching *Kids Discovery*. There was hurt over the slower than hoped for coming together, and I felt blamed. Dima was alternately quiet and accusing in regards to the changing family dynamics, but it seemed he could understand better, at times, than he had before.

When they moved into their own house, there remained energy and will within all of us to be together and develop relationship. The drama during their stay in our home had been kept minimal. One night Tatyana wept for fear that Dima and I were fighting after we had left for a walk to peaceably talk. This time I was present, on my knees, weeping beside her.

I loaded the minivan: diapers, baby food, car seats and blankets, gloves, quarters for coffee and a hot chocolate — Viktor Jr.'s and my treat before Babushka's this first snowy morning of the year. After a run through at McDonald's, I turned towards their home, the mystery of their living in America a subtle feeling, as my toddler's sing-song blended with the hum of the van.

We arrived at Babushka's and sat down to breakfast. I swallowed the dark grain cereal she served, grabbing a handful of my son's raisins and mixing familiar flavor into the kasha. I looked down at the kitchen table, mine from college, and listened as Tatyana urged Viktor Jr. to another mouthful of cereal. I felt the past sitting in our present: my mother's "Our Father" on a plaque, my aunt's fake Christmas tree with wooden ornaments my uncle had whittled before cancer. There was my mother's old couch, a symbol of adolescence and movies with Dima after Friday night football games twelve years before. Such gifts were remembrances of family past and present. With emotions attached to these images, the neutral walls of a small house became a home. However, much of these things were unfamiliar to Dima's parents, and it would take time for them to feel a part of the family and to be at home here.

I rinsed my bowl and accepted the baby from Tatyana's arms. "Moloko," I said and she nodded. I crept up the stairs to nurse the sweet-smelling infant cradled in my arms. Daylight behind curtains set the bedroom aglow. The baby was warm against my stomach. I felt comforted. I looked at their icons on the dresser and wondered how many families throughout the world and ages prayed through saints? Faith was a whisper, sometimes inaudible in the whipping winds of life. And yet it was within life and various demands that prayers blossomed.

Concrete reminders of God were necessary to reflect the purpose and meaning of life — in ways similar to things in a home reminding one of family. People, trees, the sea and sky, all creation was an icon of holiness, but to remember God by them took faith and perspective — in Christ, from Christ. Viktor's laughter drifted upstairs and the baby arched backwards, so eager to experience the world, and already distracted. I jiggled him back to me and drifted with my thoughts.

Dima's father mentioned that Americans were generous, contrary to the Soviet propaganda. It seemed easier to give from abundance — we had also been given much from family and friends — and I wondered about the gifts I felt responsible to offer that felt a high cost: time, attention, husband, children. Often, I wished instead to give a dresser, but self-sacrifice became a gift returned to me.

Of the things they weren't given, there were few things Tatyana was certain she wanted to buy. One thing she wanted was a fence around their yard. I could see how a fence might be a symbol of ownership they longed for. Fences also offered a hedge of protection, if only against the distraction of the surrounding world. Sometimes it seemed easier to separate from others, but there was often the need to relate, to connect, and no partition could extinguish this.

Being in an unfamiliar culture must have felt alienating for Dima's parents. I couldn't understand the extent of their experiences in America, but I could relate to transitioning perspective. Becoming Orthodox after having been Protestant helped me understand the difficulty in changing one's mind and way of living that both Dima's parents and my own were trying to do. While symbolic thinking was natural to me, Orthodoxy seemed to help me think more like Russian people: representatively, suggestively. Western thought tended to be different, more literal, rational, which spoke to the difficulty my parents faced in Orthodox traditions.

Allegorical thinking seemed essential to understanding for Russian people. Dima's parents' Russianness was observable in their humor, celebration, and homemaking, and I was drawn to it. They perceived and communicated life through symbols. After dinner recently, they shared a story similar to others. A friend had had too much to drink late one night but had no sick time to take off work. In hopes of getting a note from a doctor that might allow him an excuse for the next day at work, he visited the hospital. As the nurse listened to his heart with a stethoscope, he asked her how long he had to live. She replied she did not know and that she was not a coo-coo bird, whose number of "coo-coos" was thought to tell how many years a person would live. They heartily chuckled. When they arrived in America and settled into our home for the first month, a stuffed goat was set in a basket in my kitchen. Again, something was funny to the family as they pointed to the stuffed animal and called one another "goat" in a heavy accent. When Dima's father failed a driving test in America, not knowing the word "horn," his mother explained he felt like a "kettle," empty headed. If the baby was messy, he was a sweet pig; if a person learned something new, he rolled it in his mustache;

a stomach virus required a stronger spirit, vodka and salt, to free one from illness.

The Orthodox Church in America wedded cultures that could seem disparate in other situations, and it did so, in part, with language that was mystical. The way of prayer was global and eternal, rational by spiritual perspective. And yet, at St. Nicholas in Mentor, with pews, a mix of peoples — friendly, smiling and sharing doughnuts and coffee after service — my parents had left the Church after less than two years. Orthodoxy was for foreigners, some said. Some found it depressing, too somber, too restricting and wondered why one would need rules of fasting and prayer. Concentrating on aspects of the Church and missing the whole experience (not intended to be rationally understood all at once) killed the spiritual perspective, at least as much as one might know at a time, and could close one to Orthodox Christianity. In truth, it was a deeper Christian experience than any other, and, for me, the Eastern and Western coming together evident in the Church in America fortified faith.

Jesus was from the East, a Jew, but came to save all, including those quite unlike Him and His culture. Even in the time of Christ's life on earth, many of the chief priests, scribes, and elders doubted, though He performed miracles, for He didn't look or act as they had expected the promised Savior would. Their expectations came from their culture, and some were strict Jews. Culture could interfere with one's faith when it prevented changing perspective to embrace God — as He was — more fully.

Whether in Jerusalem, Russia or America, a Christian had to seek Christ with all his heart, mind, and soul, believing and hoping that in His mercy and by His grace, God would be known. Dima's parents asked very simply why my parents had left the Church. For many Russian people, if a person were Christian, they were Orthodox. I appreciated cultures that had been Orthodox for centuries. Having historic tradition more in common would be beautiful and powerful, as Russia, Greece, Romania, and other Orthodox countries had evidenced through the years in accounts of saints from these Orthodox lands. Nonetheless, faith was a personal journey, and God would call people from each land till the end of time.

After nursing for a time, Dominik fell asleep against me and we shared the afternoon peacefully at Babushkas. When it was time to leave, we seemed mutually grateful for hope that came in large part from the miracles of Viktor and Dominik.

## CHAPTER SIXTEEN

# Staying Together

I visited a monastery where an elderly nun gave me a small prayer book. In one beautiful prayer, the author offered her sadness to God:

Lift away my sadness, O Lord. In the name of the Father, and the Son, and the Holy Spirit, forgive me; I am distracted from Your will. Surrounded by thoughts of my own misery and desires for things that are not or cannot be, I cannot see how truly blessed I am.

Lift away my sadness, O Lord. Arm me with faith, and restore my sense of hope — not in others or things, but in You alone. Help me to see You, and I will not despair, for I know that the only true reason to despair belongs to those that do not know of Your love for them. Show me Your will and help me to understand.

Lift away my sadness, O Lord. Remind me that everyone has a cross to bear, even as You did. But if it is Your will, I ask that You lighten my load, for there is no hurt You cannot heal, no sin You cannot forgive, no burden You cannot ease. And although I may not understand why my load must be so heavy, reassure me that You will always help me to carry it.

Lift away my sadness, O Lord. Soften the hearts of my enemies, and be my fortress of protection from all that do not love You.

Forgive them, for their sins are not against me, but You. And if my own hand has ever caused harm, whether to another or to myself, forgive me, too, and show me the way to repair all I have done.

Lift away my sadness, O Lord. Reveal to me Your blessed reasons behind my suffering, for I do not understand them. Even more, grant me the boldness of faith that I lack, because it is only in faithfulness that true understanding comes. I am often tempted to forget that I trust You; do not ever let me forget.

Lift away my sadness, O Lord. Inspire in me a new sense of purpose. Rekindle my awareness of the love in which You created me, for You did not breathe life into me to cause me to suffer, but You promised eternal life and said to my soul, Rejoice! Hear my prayers, and help me to be patient as I wait to understand Your answers to them, all the while continuing to move forward.

Lift away my sadness, O Lord. Show me that I am not alone, my Friend and my God, and that You are always with me, even now, as I struggle to go on. My spirit is broken — Merciful Savior, fill me with Yours; For when I am filled with love for You, there will be no room in my heart for sadness. (Amelia Bacic Tulevski)

I said this prayer before going to church one Sunday, the first without my parents greeting me in the foyer with open arms to take a baby. Dima and I had fought that morning, and he'd stayed home in bed with a mild illness. My heart rang with hypocrisy. I was not "orthodox," and would never be "the right way." I could only keep trying. The icon of Mary of Egypt, written on the side wall at church, comforted me. Icons witnessed divine love, forgiveness, and change. I might also change and could feel this in communion with Mary of Egypt. God sustained each life, in every station of life.

Dima and I were struggling to stay together. I passed Fr. Andrew at coffee hour and he asked how things were going. I met his eyes with wordless pain. Some of the tension between us was explainable: I didn't serve my husband as a Russian wife might with independent ambitions. My mothering was too soft. I wanted too much control of my husband. All of this seemed a reflection of his parents' expectations meddling with his own. What it meant to be a man seemed confused by cultural tension. In addition, his parents' demand of his time and attention drained him. It seemed he blamed me for the divide between his parents and us. He seemed to want to please his parents over me. He was unwilling or unable to communicate among the variables in his life: parents, me, children, host family. As a result, and certainly only partly his fault, there was a lack of relationship among the pieces of our life. His parents were cool to me and my parents. He began accusing me of having affairs and wanting another. He craved my love, but pushed it away angrily. There were middle of the night accusations that raged through till morning, till tears and dramatic pleading that he stop, that he believe me. There was a lack of mutual trust and understanding between us. Hell.

While his parents' life contrasted the American way of life, what divided us was spiritual beyond cultural. He was unwilling to attend to Orthodox spiritual disciplines, though our mutual baptisms agreed to life in the Church. Desperation drew me to church more often where the warmth and sweet incense countered cold sinking inside. I felt divided from a man I once loved in an easier and more familiar way. One night in our bedroom, I fell to my knees before the holy icons of Christ and the Theotokos. I was silenced by layered hurt. I prayed: "Guide our thoughts and feelings and all our words and actions." Prayers were rafts keeping us above sinking. Memory of the past and hope for the future held us together as our angry words shot down peace and unity.

I rocked Dominik. Perhaps I did not need to believe when I could not. Perhaps just to be was enough, to hold my baby and feel him love me, even if I was too weak to love back, too full of my fragile, aching self. For whether I meant to see or not, before me, from within me, was a child embodying the cooperating will of man and God. Behind closed eyes, beyond the moment, I saw Dominik laughing on Dima's lap, eating a banana before bed, absorbing the ease of his father's cheek against his damp hair. A mother — more like my mom than myself — watched in the distance, easing a basket of distractions from her in a flash of acceptance. Deeper, deeper, go beyond where you are, I coaxed myself. A boy with a soft voice, a quiet knowing, dark eyes that saw through even the old in the Jewish temple where he taught. His lessons had been different than the Pharisees'. His teaching had been quiet with few and profound words. There was something perfect in his calm, like gentle waves. Dominik's breath against my chest. "What is it," I whispered in the night surrounding us.

"Jesus! Jesus!" she cried.

"What Mother?" He calmly asked. "I am in my Father's house."

Looking through the window, the moon and stars, like slits in the dark, foretold of light. I slipped the baby into the crib and went to my room where Dima was. Love was an offering: Dima and I lay on the bed in dark, candle swallowing tiny flame. I was on my back, open to his fingers tracing my abdomen, tender, holding the pain. As his touch crossed me like a whisper, I wept. All that was broken and screaming, all that was bruised and cold, warmed with his touch. There was no word to say what it meant as his voice offered: "It's going to be all right."

It was our third Lenten season when I first attempted a prayer of silence. As others discussed ways they were silencing thoughts and stilling themselves for five minutes, I couldn't imagine what I'd wrap my mind around in order not to think. However, the following day after a busy evening, children in bed, Dima downstairs waiting to continue an ongoing argument, I stopped. I collapsed into a rocking chair in the corner of our dusk-filled bedroom and concentrated on emptying my mind. I began to notice birds, a car rushing down the street, a child's laughter in the distance. This wasn't silence, I thought. But then it was so clear — each noise, each life, was in God. To notice, the self had to slip away, if only a little.

Pascha was an echo of Heaven, the unending eighth day. The Lenten journey taught one to perceive the Great Feast. Each Pascha increased my desire for the Church, for a way of life that led me deeper in faith and love, and returning to Lent was an intensified means to this always-happening end. Though I was a baby in the Faith, just as a newborn suckled and received little milk, I had what was needed, thirst.

Loving Dima was a choice, a command, and was to be sustained even in the cold. The greatest antidote to our marital strain was to experience the joy of a wedding feast in the Orthodox Church for the first time during our third Paschal tide. In the Orthodox tradition, the marriage ceremony focused on the union of Christ and his Church simultaneously with the union of a man and woman. The two people were most importantly one in Christ. They each exchanged a martyr's crown and professed death to themselves, vowing to serve one another. Each was given a sip from a cup of wine, remembering the marriage at Cana of Galilee when Christ turned water to wine. The couple's common cup of life represented the spiritual and physical reality of their union: joys would be doubled, sorrows divided.

At vespers shortly after the wedding, I faced the sunset and talked with the priest's wife outside the church. She motioned to the sunlight, "This is why Pascha is at this time of year," she said. I thought back to the first Pascha I'd experienced in the Orthodox Church as an Orthodox Christian three years earlier. It had snowed. The season had been unusually cold and dark and I had thought it insulting and deeply discouraging to celebrate "Easter" in such darkness. Especially then, I had marveled at the joy on my priest's face. It was such an ugly Sunday. Lovely weather was a blessing that encouraged good feelings and thoughts, especially poignant at Pascha, but the reality of Christ was independent of the season.

Seasons came and went and another Lenten journey was upon us. I was going to the university to teach. It was windy as I loaded the car: book bags, all day food bags, and miscellany as any such "high maintenance" (Dima had said with a laugh) woman needs for a twelve-hour teaching day. The frozen car trudged onward as I ate banana and peanut butter rice cakes. Traffic waited behind a garbage truck. In a moment was despair for another day of gray windshield winter. Hardest of all was the imminent call of my hungering self. What was it I longed for? Joyful sorrow pulsated through me: "Holy God, Holy Mighty, Holy Immortal have mercy on me." The song of silence seeped through my unconscious. I believed that miraculously, and yet so simply and constantly, the Liturgy sung at church was still singing in me. Though impossible to explain, for I did not articulate the words, did not think of them even, they were there, in the recesses of my spirit, simply because the soul recalled what was good, what was whole, despite the pains of everyday living.

Night alerted me to the state of my soul. I often woke through the night to tend my body or a child's, or, most often, to think. What such before-the-day care accomplished was worry and the obvious reality: I rejected peace, held tight to my life and to myself as proprietor of all that concerned mine. I had felt the lessening of my care in song. Sometimes words came through, but words were not the balm of comfort. Neither was the tone, the specific melody, the sound. Somehow it was something else, and something eternally deep and lasting. The feeling between Dima and me when nothing tense was between us and there was only the desire to love — this was the feeling of the song. I didn't always notice the song in me, but when it was not, I often felt the lack. I held my cross tight in my palms and prayed to be in song again. It was then I had to face what kept me from it, and the agony of changing my mind, drawing back my distracted and willful self, could keep me from peace for a time. In amazing mercy, I saw that it hadn't been long that I was kept from this mystery.

Life celebrated relationship among all things through this song. I had heard the song in Nizhny Novgorod through headphones and a Russian Orthodox choir. It was an ancient braided melody, warm as blood over the pitter patter of desire. It was a greater longing than sex, food, and personal highs. By it was the need for the world to pause, for all to be absorbed. Memory restored the song of faith in relating the past and present. My son blew dust on my computer, babbling four-year-old thoughts, making airplane sounds with a nub of pencil. Ancient Faith Radio played low from the internet, and I glanced up

*Staying Together*

at the world map above the printer. Like a seed, to seedling, to small plant, life was a chord of the song of silence.

I was slipping from the kitchen where Dima's voice followed me into the computer room where a voice on Ancient Faith Radio offered the prayer of the hour. The two voices, Dima's and the one saying a prayer, became as one. It seemed, in an instant, that words, voices, tires through rain puddles, all sounds of life bled together as prayer. Not only was each sound of life in God, but each life was entwined with all other life. This was the essence of the liturgical song that sung throughout all, even as I was perpetually swayed from hearing.

Dima and I began saying a prayer for our marriage in the evening:

> O merciful God, we beseech Thee to remind us that the married state is holy, and that we must keep it so; grant us Thy grace, that we may continue in faithfulness and love; increase in us the spirit of mutual understanding and trust, that no quarrel or strife may come between us; grant us Thy blessings, that we may stand before our fellows and in Thy sight as an ideal family; and finally, by Thy mercy, account us worthy of everlasting life: for Thou art our sanctification, and to Thee we ascribe glory: to the Father, and to the Son, and to the Holy Spirit: now and ever, and unto ages of ages. Amen.

There seemed spiritual healing between us, and we were both willing to give as much as it would take to come together and stay together.

This past Pascha, our fourth, what had changed within me was profound. I had grown more patient. Though I am indeed fully lacking in this virtue, time was not of the essence quite as it had been before. There seemed a simple acceptance in my perception. I knew the pattern: Paschal Service, Liturgy, and the feast. Towards the end of service, a young boy fainted. His eyes were glassy and his slight body unsteady as he was helped up and walked out. This was earth, not heaven, but Pascha was the closest we came to heralding the kingdom within us into our conscious experience. There was nothing at all that could happen in this world that changed the truth of holy Pascha. All would be well, and it began and ended with the soul.

We gathered in the banquet hall and Father blessed the baskets of food lining rows of tables. Dima and I had stopped at a Russian import store for goat cheese, black bread, sausage and wine. I'd met an elderly woman also preparing for Pascha that night. We purchased the same wine, and that night as Dima and I toasted to "Christ is risen! Indeed He is risen!" the wine brought me back to the woman who was somewhere celebrating with us.

During this Paschal banquet, I did not see the glow I'd seen from within Father before. I was not coddled by parishioners in quite the same way as it had seemed to me in earlier times. While it was joyful to be in mutual celebration with people I loved, the love was changed. It was deeper, truer, less superficial. It was easier, less careful, more realized. I circled the banquet hall sharing joy with many, thinking how like a wedding feast it seemed. There was weariness as at the end of a long race. I was beside Dima and his parents, eating and drinking together in celebration, and there seemed a strong root within all that was driving fast and hard into the earth.

Dima's mother's best friend from Russia came for a three-week visit this past spring. Once again, Dima traveled to New York and filled a minivan with family, bags full of tokens from his homeland, and the quiet air of transition. The feelings must have been fuzzy as Olga sat in the backseat listening to Tatyana's excited proclamation of her new home in America. She had maintained a mini Russia in her home: language—from a Russian station on the Internet, food, and décor. It had seemed to me that she had been unwilling to assimilate much of America, but with the arrival of her friend, Tatyana began acting a touch less rigidly Russian. It seemed, for the first time since their move one-and-a-half years earlier, the pride she had for her homeland began wrapping around America.

Dima returned from New York on a Sunday in late afternoon. We saddled the boys into the bicycle carrier and peddled through warming spring air, back over to his parents' for our children and me to meet Olga. She had red hair, thinner and sexier than I'd pictured. Her voice was deep and she offered a controlled chuckle often. She and Tatyana conversed as sisters do. As Olga silently sifted through her gifts from Russia, gathering small icons and toys she'd brought the boys and me, I felt the warm, earthy closeness of Dima's parents' home. There was a clutter of tea and dark bread on the counter, and the curtains were drawn despite the light that had yet to set. Breeze rustled the curtains and moved through a small living room, which also served as the family room, dining room, and, now, Olga's bedroom. I followed the boys into their room, toys tidied in the corner, small pictures of plants and children from Village Discount, and felt again the presence of God in their home.

Olga was different from Tatyana, yet they'd been friends for nearly thirty years. She looked me in the eyes with a subtle smile and offered for me to come, stay with her anytime I might travel to Russia. I felt she'd meant it. Olga easily embraced me as a woman, mother, and wife. She extended Tatyana's love to me in ways I better understood. We were family, and she didn't resist loving me for it. I had come to appreciate the unity shared with Russian people. While it was still a challenge for my independent spirit, it could be comforting to be together in such a strong way. With Olga visiting these next weeks, it was natural to feel joyful and a touch more Russian.

Tatyana put her thick arm around my small shoulders and thanked me for letting Dima travel to New York. She and the family would need Dima these next weeks, and me, she added. We'd have to drive them to stores, museums, and cities: Cleveland, Chicago, and a trip Up North. Flashbacks to their visit and initial move to the States at first left me uneasy, but it was clear that things had changed, and were changing, and that we were coming together with respect and acceptance that was nothing short of miraculous. Dima and I were light and happy and laughed with ease. We heard that those in long-lasting marriages said one thing in common: each stayed through the bad. Staying together was starting over, over and over again.

Dima's parents and Olga followed in their new car as we made our trip Up North to the Holmes'. The next day, he drove the family to nearby sand dunes. I stayed at the house, staring at the dock and rippling water. I walked, passing deer, an eagle, listening to a woodpecker in the distance. Viktor Jr. insisted woodpeckers were parrots. It was easy to mistake reality. I thought of Dominik pushing his stroller earlier that morning on a walk with Daddy and me. He'd insisted on wearing a Thomas the Train pajama top over his outfit. Bright and mismatched, he walked on his toes with the multicolored stroller. In the stroller he'd placed a piece of granola bar as his passenger. Passersby smiled and waved to Dominik, friendly and proud, swerving the stroller as he waved back.

I sat at the table before a fish puzzle when the family returned to the house. Tatyana slipped her arm around me and asked if I wanted to go to Government Island for a picnic. Late that afternoon, Dima had rented a fourteen-foot aluminum boat to ferry the family and our picnic to the island where he'd proposed ten years before. We walked through the patterned sun on the forest floor to a clearing with a picnic table and fire ring. We sat at the picnic table with raspberry vodka and small paper cups. Dima and his mother gathered wood and started the fire. As we ate, Olga told me to call her Olya, her more familiar address. Olya and Dima's mother talked and laughed, Tatyana telling me in two years we would go to Daytona Beach in Florida. I imagined us on the beach among young American bodies and laughed. Tatyana had found a Russian hotel in Daytona that gave three meals a day for $180.00. I appreciated the creative ways Dima's mother brought Russia and set her up wherever we would go.

Tatyana and Viktor seemed like young lovers as they flirted together. Viktor said, "I am around many women: my car, cat, Tatyana, and Olya." Dima's parents played together, whether cards, jokes, or swimming in the lake, even when temperatures were just above freezing. When Viktor said something, Tatyana responded passionately, sometimes arguing, sometimes biting back a smile before letting a healthy laugh shake her body. Their love was fertile soil to our family.

On this trip Up North, Dima and I shared mutual trust and understanding. In communion with one another, we laughed and were silent; we conversed and listened to the natural world around us. It felt as though a balm of wellness held us. I moved to him for a small kiss and all tensions dissolved. We walked along the road and into a plot of land for sale. Sun shined our little boys' hair as they played in the dirt. A Siberian Husky barked from the deck a house away. After some time, we turned back towards the house to grill burgers with the family.

Back in Ohio, we sat at Tatyana's dinner table for a going-away meal with Olya. Orthodoxy was connecting the dots — not in an overt or explained way — but in silent knowing. I felt the change in me and sensed it in those around me. We were steadied, accepting and joyful. Olya brought joy. We united because of her. She was a beautiful woman with a sense of humor and calm that made those around her comfortable but not bored. Shish kabobs sizzled in the garage, out of the rain, where Viktor prepared them. He brought them to the table in the enclosed patio set with various vegetables and bread, and we toasted to Olya. Viktor said they would be sad when she left, and I felt the same. Olya attempted to respond to the toast with thanksgiving to all of us, but Tatyana hushed her and said she could offer the next toast. Viktor Jr. and Dominik were wound up, spilling water from cups out of the open window. They squealed with laughter and bickered over the emptied water. Dima told them to eat the meat they pushed around on their cat head paper plates.

"The closeness we shared these three weeks is like the old days in Russia," Olya said. I slipped into the house to use the toilet. Olya stopped me in the kitchen, away from the others. She took a ring from her finger and slipped it onto mine. Speaking Russian in a tender tone, she thanked me for the time and attention we'd given her. Back at the dinner table she asked if Dima and I had friends. We nodded as she added, "You should always be one another's best friend."

It was time to leave, and we agreed to let the boys sleep over his parents'. As we were leaving Viktor said, "good luck." At first, I thought he meant good night but later wondered if maybe he understood more than I'd given him credit for. Back home, Dima and I went for a stroll down the street in a light drizzle. There was quiet calm, the best in Dima, and I was grateful for who he was and who he helped me become. I was thankful for our children, his parents and mine, and the Holmeses. That night to the Theotokos I prayed: "Raise our children to fulfill the word of God, and to be partakers of the heavenly blessedness for which they came into being."

# V

## ABSORBED BY LOVE

"For my yoke is easy and my burden is light."[*]
The Flame
Golgotha awaits you,
as do I, flesh and blood, filled with water of life.
Flush the granules of earth,
clear the sea of life that is given me,
make light what is dark: doubt to faith, hate to love,
death to life.
Your breath ignites fire from nothing, Wordless Wisdom.
You embalm a world that doesn't feel Your touch.
Flame of fury, fire of truth, emblazon all that is Yours.

---

[*] The Orthodox Study Bible, New King James Version, First edition, (Nashville: Thomas Nelson Publishers, 1997), Matt 11:30.

**CHAPTER SEVENTEEN**

# Our Fifth Pascha: Passover from Death to Life

Central to Christian faith was Pascha, the resurrection of Christ by which all would rise again in life, reconciled to incorruption before from the fall of Adam. The Passion of Christ was paradoxical: God as man, life by death; bright sadness and radiant darkness. On this day, the unending eighth day, God's miracles continued[1]: He created the world from nothingness, delivered the Israelites from Pharaoh and through the Red Sea, and descended from heaven and filled the virgin Mary's womb. By Pascha, Christ trampled on death by death and upon those in the tombs bestowed life. But, what was Pascha? The manifestation of "divine warmth [and] life-giving brightness" (174).

It was an Easter celebration with our family, 2010, and Easter and Pascha coincided this year. Family wondered how the long night went with the children. I was happy to be together with family in the Holmes' grand home. Ten people talked around a center island before dinner tasting salmon, cheese, and crackers. In the works was dinner: roasted asparagus, a mound of sweet ham, salads and fruit, potatoes, chocolates — and a tall cheesecake, "pascha." The mood was light and joyful, and when my aunt asked me about the night before, beyond the marvels of our two small boys' bedtime at four in the morning after "a big, big party," as three-year-old Dominik had shared, I paused. What was Pascha? For the answer was in the deep spiritual joy that

---

[1] Fr. David Kidd and Mother Gabriella Ursache, eds., *Synaxarion of the Lenten Triodion and Pentecostarion*, (Rivers Junction: HDM Press, 2003), 163–174.

surpassed even good things on earth. There was always hope because there was always love, and this truth came from Pascha. Father Alexander Schmemann explained:

> We are no longer people in meaningless time that leads to a meaningless end. We are given not only a new meaning in life, but even death itself has acquired a new significance. In the troparion of Pascha we say, 'trampling down death by death.' We do not say that He trampled down death by the Resurrection, but by death. And although a Christian still faces death, being in this way similar to any other man, death has for him a new significance. It means entering into the Pascha of the Lord, into His own passage from the old into a new life. This is the key to the liturgical year of the Church. Christianity is, first of all, the proclamation in this world of Christ's Resurrection. Orthodox spirituality is paschal in its inner content, and the real content of the Christian life is joy.[2]

Via the Internet, I saw a picture of a Romanian woman weeping beside a grave on Pascha night. Small fires were about the graveyard, defeating the dark, symbols of Christ's victory over all sin and its capstone, death. She wore a beautiful silk head covering, her body was thick and old, and there was a strange feeling as I observed our different stations in life. I was self-conscious of how little the reality of Christ's victory over death affected me. The joy that I saw over this woman's entire body reminded me of the joy I had seen on Fr. Andrew's face my first Pascha.

By the grace of God, spiritual joy seemed to be increasing in me. This past Lent, I sensed more acutely what the Church calls bright sadness or joyful sorrow. It seemed great joy struggled against simultaneous irritations and earthly cares. On Good Friday, I whispered to

---

[2] Alexander Schmemann, "Holy Pascha," *A Liturgical Explanation of Holy Week*, <http://www.groupsrv.com/religion/about326639.html> (7 April 2010).

a couple in front of me: "The soul is fragile. This service is stilling." We approached the tomb where Christ lay. We bowed down, kissed His feet, the Gospel, His shoulder.

On Pascha night, though they had napped from eight to eleven, our children were spinning with energy as the night progressed, which often happened when they moved past exhaustion. Some said the boys' laughter and unbridled joy encouraged them. I tried to understand as I picked up and ran after too-energized small bodies. Christ said we must receive the kingdom of God like a child, and, as Fr. Alexander said, "To become like a child, in Christ's words, means to be capable of that joy of which an adult is no longer capable, to enter into communion with things, with nature, with other people, without suspicion or fear or frustration." Joy was the reference point from which everything else must be understood.[3] Just before midnight, the church was full and expecting in silence as the priest's candle illumined another's and so forth until we held flames and softly sang, "Your resurrection, O Christ our God, the angels in heaven sing, enable us on earth, to glorify You in purity of heart," processing around the church.

In the banquet hall, there seemed a sea of new faces (we'd begun attending a parish nearer to home six months before). As I wondered with whom we'd sit, Dominik ate an egg and its red shell. I wanted wine. We were invited by a woman to sit and feast, and her Pascha baskets were packed with fine goods: bacon, deviled eggs, various sweets. She asked what I'd made as I offered some blueberry bread (from the box). "My son's favorite," I meekly added. On the drive home, I was nauseous. The bottle of wine spilled on my white skirt. There was something more, however, something continuing to bob its head up inside. Joy. Spiritual joy that assured me that even here and now, even in this imperfect world, "Christ is risen from the dead!" There would come a day when perfect joy would be realized without compromise, and God willing I'd be a part of the grand feast

---

[3] Ibid.

along with everyone who chose to believe and accept the greatest gift imaginable! Dima and I held tightly onto one another's hands just before dawn.

I entered the unending eighth day for a slow jog. Birds flitted between trees and squirrels over fresh grass. I woke Dima with a kiss. He stared out the window and asked me if I noticed how the weather seemed to match the events of these days. On Holy Saturday, after a sunny day, the evening grew dark and stormy, as Christ was in hades freeing Adam and those who believed from the bondage of death. When we left church around six, the sky had cleared and it was still and peaceful. This Pascha day, though it was forecasted to be rainy, was radiant. After eggs and potatoes and sweet coffee, we ventured outside with our boys. Looking into the sky, Dima noticed a rainbow in a perfect circle around the sun. "It's a sign, you choose to believe or not," he said. I believed, encouraged through the experience of Pascha.

Though the unending eighth day was passed in a physical sense, Resurrection Sunday tapped into the cycle of salvation continuously. Silently, I continued to beseech the Lord to enable me to glorify Him. I wondered how to celebrate Pascha on the Wednesday of Bright Week. I was not familiar with the cycle of prayers that professed celebration on the days following Pascha when Christians do not prostrate, fast, or pray to the Holy Spirit, as Christ was among us, walking and laughing and rejoicing in the salvation of the world. Before breakfast, the children and I sang, "Christ is risen from the dead, trampling down death by death, and upon those in the tombs bestowing life!" I tried to realize what this meant in light of a day when I was weary and children had unending needs. When Dima returned from work, we ventured to the park with our boys, throwing a football and laughing. We returned to ham and cheesy potatoes, wine and homemade pickles, and, finally, bedtime. As a family, we sang, "Your resurrection, O Christ our God, the angels in heaven sing, enable us on earth, to glorify You in purity of heart," and the children drifted to sleep.

What was Pascha? His grace and mercy born from love, sprinkling me no less than the Romanian woman who may have known

Him longer, who likely lived more piously in a culture more Orthodox than America. Various ways of loving in each culture with the means available to each one: money, talents, opportunities expressed faith. Purity of heart from living for God developed faith. By faith, God's gift, one could believe in His glorious resurrection. I could believe in my own someday. "On this day of resurrection, be illumined O people! Pascha, the Pascha of the Lord! From death to life, and from earth to heaven, has Christ our God led us, singing the song of victory: Christ is risen from the dead!"[4]

---

[4] First Ode of the Paschal Canon.

## CHAPTER EIGHTEEN

# Soul Laughter: Joy in My Heart

St. John the Theologian Monastery was nested in a rural suburb nearby. Two monks lived there. It was Paschal tide of our fifth Pascha when I came for service and breakfast. The day was unusually hot. I told Viktor to stay in his car seat while I moved to the back of the van for candle stubs the monks would melt and reuse. The sun was against bare shoulders as I slipped into a thin sweater. Father met me on the driveway before the garage. I said I could get the few boxes from the van and set them in the garage. He was patient, kind, paused to listen to me laugh over an anecdote, and returned without much delay to light candles, prepare incense, and ready hymns for service. Fresh Pascha flowers and palm branches added to the sanctuary he and the abbot had spent over eight hours readying for Pascha service. They had polished brass, adorned icons with flowers, shook rugs and dusted wood. Ancient windows were carefully cleaned, and the entire place, already full of the presence of God, was made even more beautiful and inviting by removing some of what naturally collected in this life. Despite the abbot's crippled feet and Father's ailing back, they worked for the glory of God—sometimes only God and a few others that happened to be there with them. Over cheesy eggs, fish, and endless sweet breads, I learned they had only two people physically in service Pascha night. Their work of beautifying the sanctuary, just as efforts made in purifying their souls, was ultimately for God — and all the invisible hosts who accompanied Him. What I saw in their eyes as we ate was happiness.

Three weeks later, I headed to an evening writing class I taught. Jazzy music, perfume, fast-walking youth on cell phones wearing flip flops: I had entered The Strip. At this chain of stores and eateries, I would meet students at Panera Bread for their final presentations. I passed a mother and her small son feeling slower than usual, lingering empty-hearted in a distant childhood. As a child, vision was softer and Nana bought me school clothes and peanut butter cup cookies, a thick swirl of fudge being nothing but pleasure I accepted. Somewhere along this way of growing up and moving on — past indulgent grandmothers and into marriage and children — I had forgotten the freeing joy of happiness. Joy was there, the deep goodness and full blaze of promise that God loved me, I loved Him, and the worth of life could be shared lovingly with others. What seemed harder to tap into was like the fudge atop the peanut butter cup: the extra tasty treat that made me smile.

A student read a creative piece of writing intended as a sort of poetic letter to her boyfriend. The girl wore canary sandals and a summer dress despite the cool air. She shared how she had discovered love. Her forehead shone, curly hair about a round face, and she read: "I wanted you to want to know me."

I offered, "From now on and through marriage, want, instead, to know him." Love flourished with small steps towards the other: God, my Dima. One worked to care for the details of another's life, to bring them coffee with two teaspoons of sugar, to pause and offer a kiss before moving on to the dishes. What happened after honeymoons seemed a reversal of what allowed the love to flourish in the beginning: one stopped getting to know the other and wanted more to be understood.

How I treated Dima was the greatest witness of Christ's changing me. Love was cooperation with God. As Fr. David Moser[1] said, "Our task is the acquisition of the Holy Spirit (St. Seraphim), our task is the

---

[1] *Eastern Orthodox Christian Evangelism is Different*, www.orthodox.net/articles/evangelism.html, 20 April 2010.

working out of our salvation, our task is to repent and weep for our sins, our task is to enter the kingdom of God." Usually, when one gave love, one was given love — for love was as a circle, the center of which was joy.

The greatest calling I had was to teach my children to know God, and to show them such love in my responses to Dima. My patron saint, Lea, fourth century, was widowed and went into a monastery where she became a superior. She wore no makeup and humbled herself to obey others. She denied the pull of the body and found life in the spirit. She increased in faith and power. Ultimately, it was said that she enjoyed perfect happiness as a fool for Christ.

I speedily sneaked the frozen meat into the microwave as Dima changed his clothes before our family cookout. He came into the kitchen wearing a shirt from our honeymoon to Maui ten years before. It was grass green and clashed against ancient gray cutoffs. Day was slipping to dusk. It was Resurrection Sunday. Dima's parents were the first to arrive for Dominik's birthday party. Deydushka came with a hockey net and immediately set up game on the driveway. He offered the first toast to our son. "For health, happiness, that he listen and obey his parents." A pregnant pause. "That he respect the elderly." We drank.

I appreciated Deydushka's genuine heart and willingness to love us. I appreciated Russian culture with simple things like birthday toasts. I hoped that Dima's parents appreciated the culture of open-mindedness in America. It seemed to me a willingness to consider others' perspectives was very possible in American culture and could be the means through which truth was heard. It was up to each individual to tend to truth or to reject it, but saints were made in every place and through all times. People were to learn from each other, accept one another, and recall Christ. So long as this was so, simple moments shared might lead to common ground — to shared life in Christ. I laughed with Dima as we split a burger.

It was a day of errands with the children, and it was good to be together. In the minivan, my children sang a song from nursery school:

"I've got the joy, joy, joy, joy down in my heart — Where? — down in my heart — Where? — down in my heart!" And I joined in, recalling the song from my childhood. To be as children, accepting and open, was the only way to experience joy and, ultimately, salvation. If we knew this experience, meditated upon it, lived with it guiding our thoughts and feelings, then those about us would search the well, and we'd be encouraged and learn to feel love again.

Joy lit inside as Dima and I readied our sons for bed that night. Daddy wrestled with little Dominik: open-mouth laughter, white teeth, blond hair. I cuddled with Viktor, calming him from the day's energy: soccer, swimming, laughing with his brother. I tickled his small arms and studied the skin around his eyes slightly taut with sun and weariness. He would grow and go. I felt the slippery moment as he whispered, "I miss you, Momma," falling into sleep.

When things were going well, peace with others might be taken for granted, but it was always a gift to have mutual understanding and trust. After a time of sorrow, one more naturally realized this. As a marriage deepened, there was much to work through, but when two people chose love, found again and again in Christ's own life, joy was found, and it was deep and enduring.

Marriages often failed, but it was possible to stay together. It may take another moment, or another day, but faith in Dima was possible. On Sunday, our family went to church and partook of Holy Communion. A balm of calm came over Dima and me. We were soft and quiet and looked into each other's eyes. I would never leave. He would never leave. He held me gently, with great love, and what I felt in that moment was a miracle. I was numb to all but the purest, surest love.

I stayed up late watching a documentary on an English brain surgeon. He worked in Ukraine, offering free medical advice and even surgeries for those who had been told there was no hope, there was no way to alleviate their pain, and, many times, their impending deaths. He was a remarkable man, generous and caring, but also honest and seeking. He knew when death was the winner. He commented on the adrenaline felt before an operation, saying complacency was the worst thing for a surgeon to experience before a surgery. At the end of the program, the doctor visited a family who had lost a daughter after a surgery he'd performed. The dinner was set out just as Russian meals I'd shared with family and friends: toasts of vodka, dishes of small- chopped salads, fine china, crystal decanters and delicate tea cups. Afterwards, the doctor walked through a graveyard alone. He said when he dies, if anything were on his mind, it would likely be this girl and her family. He concluded life was about helping others. Each was called by God to do what they could in this world to foster love. I wept with desire to do something to help others.

It seemed those most remarkable were willing to help others even when it was a cost to themselves. People like my parents' friends, the Georgeses, who continued to help children in Uganda. In a recent newsletter, they shared how a Ugandan brother and sister had been accepted into their school program. After a short time, the brother had to stop school and work, as they were very poor and he hadn't done well on a test that would qualify him for secondary education. The boy's hope persisted, and upon retaking the test, he was able to continue school with his sister on scholarship. These children, as many like them, were without family (due to disease and poverty) and often without food and shelter. Education was a privilege, made possible by Americans willing to head a nonprofit organization and continue a mission in love.

I considered my lot was to love my family and serve them. Impossible turnarounds were made possible by love that looked beyond the ugliness of pain and present problems and hoped in life. Each person was changing and capable of sanctification. The nature of life was fragile, and yet roots were always growing and knotting firm in the earth. It was difficult to pull forth the tree of life, designed to live in the conditions in which it was planted. Cultivating faith in God fertilized each with love that allowed blossoms of joy, despite the pains that came. People moving in and out of my life, weaving the fabric of new experience, challenged me with the always near option of love. I crossed myself and turned to the window where my children beckoned me outside.

Transfigured sorrow was spiritual joy. I understood more now how the mark of a Christian was joy. It wasn't necessarily that life would always be happy. However, a Christian's response to anything that happened in life was to pray to God, accepting His will and enduring it, and experiencing hope. A Christian had a mission in life to love others. It was not always easy, but sometimes it was. Just like marriage. We were to become one, to learn that life was not all about me, and to laugh a little along the way.

Through Dima, Grandma, Viktor and Tatyana, I entered the Faith. By the Faith our family would stay together. The glue was Love, was Christ Himself, and it was He that connected the dots of our family. Lord have mercy, always and forever.